ADVANCE PR

"One of the biggest misconceptions about atheists is that without God they can have no morals, values, or meaning in their lives. In this lovely secular sermon, Dan Barker handily rebuts that claim, showing that *true* meaning and morality can come only from accepting our finitude, and dealing with it rationally and humanistically."

—**Jerry Coyne**, Professor of Ecology and Evolution, University of Chicago, and author of *Why Evolution Is True*

"Dan Barker has cleverly reversed the arrows of purpose so they fly from the bows of life instead of raining down from an imaginary archer in the sky."

—**Victor J. Stenger**, author of *God: The Failed Hypothesis*

"If you've been searching for meaning and purpose in life, it's a sure bet you've never found answers in a book—at least not answers that are grounded in any kind of objective reality—until now. Dan Barker's *Life Driven Purpose* deserves its own category. It's a book of emancipation, a book of vitality, a book of enrichment, a book of celebration, a book of inspiration—put simply, a book that honestly and rationally teaches how to live."

—**Peter Boghossian**, author of *A Manual for Creating Atheists*

"Religions hijacked the meaning of life long ago and now Dan Barker is stealing it back. In this brilliant and inspirational book, he shows that value, worth, and meaning can be discovered and created by anyone—no religion required."

—**Guy P. Harrison**, author of *Think: Why You Should Question Everything* and *50 Simple Questions for Every Christian*

"This book is really 'Something' (see chapter 5). In his calm, patient voice, Dan Barker helps us understand and untwist black-and-white thinking so we can see and appreciate all the colors of the rainbow."

—**Linda LaScola**, coauthor (with Daniel Dennett) of *Caught in the Pulpit: Leaving Belief Behind*

"*Life Driven Purpose* is an important book that puts the lie to the strange notion that without God life has no purpose. Living is great, fulfilling, and meaningful without God. Like his previous book, *Godless*, *Life-Driven Purpose* is a book that every one with an interest in spirituality, religion in political life, and how to lead a meaningful life will want to have on their shelves."

—**Daniel Everett**, author of *Don't Sleep, There Are Snakes* and *Language*

"Dan says he's certainly not pretending to be a Deacon of Atheism or Bishop of Freethought, but he is. In this book Deacon Dan uses good scholarship in offering convincing answers to some of the most important reasons why believers keep on believing despite the lack of sufficient evidence. Writing with the wit and storytelling of a preacher, this series of 'sermons' will definitely reach the masses. I heartily endorse it. May it produce a revival, one of reason, logic, and science."

—**John W. Loftus**, author of *Why I Became An Atheist, The Outsider Test for Faith*, and coauthor of *God or Godless?*

"Deftly handling the complexities of philosophy and physics, meaning and morality, Barker debunks the woefully inadequate monochromatic worldview of the religious fundamentalist and replaces it with one of rich color and beauty. This accessible, witty, and thoughtful book provides answers to the most profound questions but, more than that, it helps us embrace life; life in all its fullness."

—**Paul Beaumont**, author of *A Brief Eternity*

"In *Life Driven Purpose* Dan Barker confronts the complexities of moral behavior and offers us the gift of his lifelong engagement with the Big Questions. Everyone will profit from reading Barker's penetrating and revealing analyses, but the true believers will profit most, since they have the most to lose, and to gain. One of Barker's advantages in wrestling with these profound issues is that for many years he was himself one of the true believers, preaching the orthodox gospel—so he knows the tricks of the trade; he's been inside the orthodox stronghold, and knows where the bodies are buried. Barker is not only smart, he is wise, and this book is an invaluable gift to all of us."

—**Philip Appleman**, Distinguished Professor Emeritus, Indiana University

LIFE DRIVEN PURPOSE

LIFE DRIVEN PURPOSE
How an Atheist Finds Meaning

DAN BARKER

FOREWORD BY DANIEL C. DENNETT

PITCHSTONE PUBLISHING
Durham, North Carolina

Pitchstone Publishing
Durham, North Carolina 27705
www.pitchstonepublishing.com

To contact the publisher, please e-mail info@pitchstonepublishing.com

Printed in the United States of America

10 9 8 7 6 5 4 3 2 1

Library of Congress Cataloging-in-Publication Data

Barker, Dan.
  Life driven purpose : how an atheist finds meaning / Dan Barker ; foreword by
Daniel C. Dennett.
      pages cm
  Includes bibliographical references and index.
  ISBN 978-1-939578-21-1 (pbk. : alk. paper)
  1. Life. 2. Conduct of life. 3. Ethics. 4. Atheism. I. Title.
  BD431.B2788 2014
  211'.8—dc23
                            2013049775

Cover photo by Ingrid Laas

For Anne Nicol Gaylor
who shows us how to live
a purpose-filled life

CONTENTS

FOREWORD

"What is the point of my life?" This question cannot have haunted many people in earlier centuries; they were too busy scratching out a living, providing food and shelter for their families, fending off threats to their health and security. But now that we have pretty well solved the most pressing problems of staying alive, and have the free time to reflect on what it all means, we are assaulted at every turn by a flood of information about the apparently meaningful lives of a lucky few—doctors, judges, guitar heroes, sports stars, billionaires, celebrities, politicians, explorers of ocean depths, and conquerors of the highest mountains. If we can't all have glamorous lives—if we can't all be famous for even fifteen minutes—what is the point, really? Why should we care about anything?

The best answer today has been the best answer for millennia: find something more important than you are, and devote your life to it, protecting it, improving it, making it work, celebrating it. But doesn't this usually require joining forces with others, finding a supporting organization with a clear vision? Yes, it does, and for centuries the premier options have been religions, made all the more irresistible by one of the great master strokes of advertising: *you can't be good without God.* There may well have been a time when this was practically true, when the only feasible path to a life of importance (and we all want our lives to be important) was to be a member in good standing of one church or another, one temple or another. Step One in the project of having a meaningful life was to be *God-fearing*. Those who weren't God-fearing were seen as disreputable, untrustworthy, sinful, defective, empty.

The term "God-fearing" is a fascinating fossil trace of earlier times, when the standard or default conception of God was as an anthropomorphic Protector of Us (but not Them), Merciful Judge, Witness to our sins, Appreciator of our praise and our incessant declarations of undying loyalty. And that largely obsolete conception of God was itself a direct descendant of earlier conceptions of gods that were genuinely frightening, because they had to be appeased, and were far from loving or just or even good. How strange that the term should survive today with so little recognition of not only its obsolescence but its embarrassing history of oppression!

Wake up, folks! Listen to what your holy texts actually say! Among the delights of Dan Barker's book are the succession of startling juxtapositions, looking at our religious practices through the eyes of a quizzical Martian. Did you realize that all Christian ministers are essentially slave traders, prized for their ability to soothe and cajole their flock of slaves into ever more submissive obedience, and even getting them to pay their keepers?

> Asking, "If there is no God, what is the purpose of life?" is like asking, "If there is no Master, whose slave will I be?" If the purpose of life is to become a submissive slave, then your meaning comes from flattering the ego of a person whom you should despise.

The historical Jesus is nicely compared to the historical Paul Bunyan. (Was there a huge lumberjack in the North Woods who inspired the tales? Maybe. Does it matter?) Then there is Barker's darker demonstration of how religion compromises our moral judgment, by telling a story of utter depravity and eliciting a judgment from an audience that this was the deed of a moral monster, and then changing the names and circumstances oh so slightly and turning it into the horrific tale in the book of Job. As Richard Dawkins has so vividly and memorably put it, in *The God Delusion,*

> The God of the Old Testament is arguably the most unpleasant character in all fiction: jealous and proud of it; a petty, unjust, unforgiving control-freak; a vindictive, bloodthirsty ethnic cleanser; a misogynistic, homophobic, racist, infanticidal, genocidal, filicidal, pestilential, megalomaniacal, sadomasochistic, capriciously malevolent bully.

Some people have found this assertion unforgivably rude, but if they pause to reflect on what the tales from the Old Testament, read literally, actually tell us, how can they not acknowledge that it is a fair assessment? Barker's ingenious exercises of imagination draw the point to our attention in a more playful spirit than Dawkins' blunt condemnation, but the message is the same. And the broader conclusion to draw is that a religion that cannot survive looking at itself through the eyes of others does not deserve to survive.

Barker is so good at this because he is intelligent and honest and has had lots of practice. As a former minister himself, he has an intimate knowledge not only of the Bible but of all the ways that clergy and their congregations subliminally conspire to blur their own vision when confronting the flaws in their traditions. He does not shrink from acknowledging the bleak prospect, even the terror, of letting go of all the paternalistic pabulum and becoming a grownup. But then he shows how surprisingly easy it is to be a good person! Yes, you can learn to ride a bike, and yes, you can become a good and meaningful person without bothering yourself with all the dark confusions and contradictions imposed on you by your heritage of irrationality and obfuscation.

> We don't need religion to be good. Religion actually gets in the way. Getting rid of purely religious mandates makes life simpler and safer.

Rejecting religion filters out the noise to bring a clarity of judgment, making it easier to be a good atheist than a good Christian.

We all want to find purpose in our lives. Pastor Rick Warren, in his best-seller *The Purpose Driven Life*, designed an eloquent and subtle advertisement for subjecting yourself to the demands of Christianity, and without a doubt there are thousands of feckless young people who discovered thereby the discipline and self-respect to turn themselves into good citizens of the world, responsible and caring—but at a huge price: blinding themselves to the possibility of other good lives (for their purpose must be converting the world to Warren's brand of Christianity) and to all the hard-won discoveries of science (and history and literature) that contradict the Christian message.

Former pastor Dan Barker has designed an equally eloquent and subtle antidote in *Life Driven Purpose*, showing us by example how a very good person can get along fine without religion, inspiring others, accomplishing great works, and having a lot of fun in the bargain.

—**Daniel C. Dennett**
Tufts University

INTRODUCTION

"Life is meaningless without God!"

How many times have I heard that? I have participated in more than a hundred public debates and have listened to many arguments for the existence of God, and often my opponents will throw in this nonargument during closing statements. "You may not be convinced by the evidence and arguments," they admit, "but you should believe anyway because otherwise your life is empty and worthless."

That rhetoric may work for some, but not for me. Tens of millions of people in the United States, and hundreds of millions around the world, lead happy, loving, productive, moral, and meaningful lives without believing in a god. We atheists have immense purpose—life-driven purpose—thank you, and are not starving for anything more.

I do not pretend to speak for all atheists. The subtitle of this book is "How *an* Atheist Finds Meaning," not "How All Atheists Find Meaning." Each atheist is an individual, not part of a religion or creed. We do not agree with each other on all issues, nor should we. Atheism is simply the absence of theism. Atheists do not have a religious belief; we lack a belief in God or gods, and that is the only thing that unites us. (We might possess beliefs about other things, but we don't have a belief in a god.) But I am certain that the views I express in this book are shared to a very large degree by most atheists on the planet. I have talked with thousands of them. I have read the writings of many hundreds more. To be sure, a small handful of atheists (including some well-known philosophers) are existential nihilists who think life has no meaning and ultimately ends in despair and emptiness. My religious opponents like to quote those pessimists, pretending that they speak for all of us. The cheery Schopenhauer, for example, said that the only thing better than suicide is never to have been born in the first place. I don't share that view, and I don't know any atheists who do. The atheists I know, virtually all of whom are happy and mentally healthy, might more properly be called anti-nihilists. We are mainly optimists who love our lives and find them to be full of meaning and purpose.

I am not going to prove atheism or disprove religion or Christianity in this book. I attempt that elsewhere, especially in my books *Losing Faith in Faith: From Preacher to Atheist* and *Godless: How an Evangelical Preacher Became One of America's Leading Atheists.* A wealth of criticism of faith can be found in the capable writings of many other informed atheists (see bibliography). I will critique some aspects of the religious mind-set regarding purpose and meaning, but will set aside atheist arguments for the most part. This book assumes the reasonableness of atheism and then takes it from there.

The main chapters of *Life Driven Purpose* are the first and last. Chapter 1, "The Good News," deals with purpose, and chapter 5, "Life is Life," deals with meaning. (Some of the material in chapter 1 appeared in a different form in my book *The Good Atheist.*) If you had to skip the middle essays—please don't!—you would walk away with the take-home message that atheists indeed lead rich and meaningful lives, that there are good reasons for this, and that life as a nonbeliever can be *better* than life as a believer.

You may have found *Life Driven Purpose* in the "Inspirational" section of the bookstore and were surprised to see an atheist book there. Well, I think we nonbelievers are the ones who are truly "in-spired."

Believers are "out-spired." We atheists find purpose and create meaning within ourselves.

Chapter 2, "Mere Morality," lays out my views on human behavior. It is my way to answer the question, "How can we be good without God?" I don't expect believers to applaud, nor do I expect all atheists to agree with my approach, but I do expect you to acknowledge that if at least one coherent secular naturalistic moral philosophy can be articulated, then nobody can honestly claim that adhering to religion or theism is the only way to be good, or the only way to objectively justify moral behavior.

Although chapter 3, "Religious Color Blindness," does deal with purpose and meaning, it is mainly an attempt to understand the mind of a fundamentalist. If you are an atheist, I hope this will help you talk with a true believer. If you are one of those true believers, then I hope it will allow you to see yourself from a different point of view. It might explain why we appear to be talking at cross-purposes, and help you understand why I would change my mind after nineteen years of preaching the Gospel.

Chapter 4, "Much Ado About," is my attempt to answer the question, "Can something come from nothing?" or "Why is there something rather than nothing?" These are not arguments for the existence of a god—they are just questions—but they are interesting and relevant, and many believers imagine they prove something. I make what I think is a strong case that those distracting questions are fruitless. I intend for this chapter to remove a prop from the claim that we were created by a superior intelligence to serve his aims rather than our own. It is not directly related to purpose and meaning, except for the fact that if there weren't something rather than nothing, there could be no meaning or purpose at all!

It is true that "atheism" is a negative word, but so is "nonfiction." They are double negatives. Both words tell you that what you are getting is *real*, not pretend. Those of us who do not believe in a god have nothing to be ashamed of, nothing to fear, and nothing to regret over our lack of faith. On the contrary, we nonbelievers have something valuable to offer the world, underscoring the fact that life is valuable for its own sake alone. Unlike many believers, we atheists are not smug, divisive, or exclusive about our views: we welcome all people into the natural human family. A supernatural additive pollutes what is pure and precious in our species. We atheists simply refuse to be cheated of the good life.

* * *

A note about usage. Although it is commonly accepted practice to capitalize "Bible," my personal style is to write "bible," unless it is the name of a specific book, such as the King James Bible, or appears in a quote. This is not disrespectful: it is un-respectful. We do the same with "dictionary," which we only capitalize in the names of actual books, such as *Merriam Webster Dictionary*. Note that the adjective "biblical" is lowercase, while the adjectives of actual proper names are not: Victorian, Darwinian, Grecian. Dan Dennett uses "Bible" in his Foreword, which shows that we atheists are free to disagree in matters of personal choice.

1

THE GOOD NEWS

It *is* about you.

Forget what pastor Rick Warren says. When it comes to purpose, it is about you and no one else.

This doesn't mean *everything* is about you. Morality is how you treat your neighbor and truth is how well your statements match reality. Behavior and opinions can actually be objectively right or wrong, independent of your thoughts.

But purpose is personal. It can't be right or wrong. It can't be true or false. It can't *not* be about you. It's how *you* decide to live your own life. If someone else tells you how to live, you are not free. If you don't choose your own purpose, you are a slave.

In a few pages, I am going to tell you the truly good news about purpose, the surprising and perhaps counterintuitive message that atheists offer to the world. I will explain exactly how we nonbelievers find or create meaning, and why the uplifting, edifying, and self-actualized stance of atheism is superior to the irrelevant and impoverished world view of god believers.

When I was a Christian minister, I thought it was the other way around. "The fool hath said in his heart, 'There is no God,'" I believed.[1]

I imagined atheism was bankrupt and depressing. I preached the "good news" from John 3:16: "For God so loved the world that he sent his only begotten son, that whoever believes in him should not perish but have everlasting life." On its face, that sounds very special—love, belief, escaping death, everlasting life—but what does it actually mean? What is this great evangelical news that we are supposed to be excited about?

Suppose you are walking by my house, and I come out on my front porch and say:

Hey! I've got some good news!

Stop! Listen! This is great news! You've been passing by every day and you have been ignoring me. I love you, and I have so much to offer you. I am special, and I am worthy of admiration. You can't keep walking by as if I don't even exist. So I have some good news for you:

You don't have to go down in my basement!

That's right. This is great news, because since you have been ignoring me all these years, and have not been giving me the proper respect I deserve, you have made me very upset. I become an angry person when I am not honored, when my loving character is not appreciated.

So, I built a torture chamber down in my basement.

It's dark and hot down there, with sharp knives and chains and hooks on the walls, and a furnace with flames, and some smelly vats with caustic Lake-of-Fire chemicals. It's horrible. But the good news is that you don't have to go down there.

I sent my son down there.

It was ugly. It was horrific. My only-begotten son experienced an agony of suffering and shame.

But that satisfied my anger, and I'm not mad any more. It is finished. And that is great news for you! All you have to do is come up here on my porch and thank my bleeding son for what he did for you. Tell him you love him. We'll forgive your arrogance. Give us a big hug, and come into my house, and we'll live up in the attic together, and you can spend an eternity of gratitude telling me How

Great I Am, while your ingrate friends and relatives are screaming down in the basement. Won't that be wonderful?

Isn't this just the best news you have ever heard?

So, what would you do? Would you keep walking?

That is Christianity in a nutshell. It is ghastly news. Ignore it. Keep walking and get on with your life.

"What is the purpose of life?" is a slippery question because purpose has more than one meaning. In its primary usage—the one relevant to living beings—purpose is striving for a goal, an intentional aiming at a target. There is no striving without a reason, and the reason always has something to do with surviving or enjoying your life. If you are not enjoying life—or striving to enjoy life—you are not living your life. Enjoyment doesn't exist for its own sake; *you* exist for your own sake. Enjoyment results from successfully reaching or striving to reach a goal.[2]

The goal can be to get something you want, or to avoid something you don't want. The purpose of your actions might be the need for food, water, or shelter. It might be to find a mate, or repel a threat. It might be physical exercise, to keep fit to meet future challenges. These goals, and others, when achieved by some kind of striving, are pleasurable or positive, because they ultimately relate to survival. Less tangible goals, such as beauty, love, friendship, learning, adventure, and entertainment—and these all have risks as well as rewards—are enjoyable when obtained because they contribute to well-being, which enhances survival. Even indirect goals, such as helping others to survive, are enjoyable. (More about that in chapter 2.) They all affect the brain, which is a physical organ striving to control and protect a natural organism in a natural environment.

That is your life. That is what purpose means. Life is purpose, and purpose is life.

Purpose also has a secondary usage, which is what we mean when we transfer a goal to the method used to achieve that goal. When we ask for the purpose of a hammer, we are not imagining that a tool has any intentions. We are really asking for the purpose in the mind of the person who designed or uses the hammer. The hammer was invented by organisms with opposable thumbs as a way to deliver a large direct force to the head of a nail (not to the opposable thumb), driving it into wood, or to leverage the force to yank it back out. It was designed to help construct things like shelter, bridges, and military defenses, all having something to do with survival. If you didn't know what a hammer was, you might be able to reverse-engineer and guess its primary purpose, but you might also use it for something else, perhaps as a juggling toy, or to strike a musical instrument, or as a weapon. The purpose of a tool does not come from within itself. It comes from within a living mind striving to enhance survival. It is only living things that possess purpose. When we ask, "What is the purpose of a hammer?" we assume that the hammer is lifeless.

So asking, "What is the purpose of life?" assumes that life is dead. The question hinges on an equivocation that comes from confusing two different usages of purpose. Since purpose is life, asking for the purpose of life is like asking, "What is the life of life?" That question is based on a belief that life, like a tool, has no internal purpose of its own. If you don't have the freedom to choose to strive for your own goals, then you are not really alive. You are a hammer. If you think your purpose must come from outside yourself, you are a lifeless implement or a slave to another mind.

And that is exactly what most religions teach. The so-called good news of Christianity, for example, cheats its followers with the sleight of hand of trading purpose for purpose, euthanizing the individual by cutting out the heart of life and implanting it elsewhere. It turns a living creature into a dead shell.

The apostle Paul taught exactly this, that we are empty clay pots: "But we have this treasure in earthen vessels, that the excellency of the power may be of God, and not of us."[3] He told believers to "Present your bodies as a living sacrifice, holy and acceptable to God."[4] Those words were written by a man who called himself a "slave" of Christ: "I have been crucified with Christ. It is no longer I who live, but Christ who lives in me."[5] "For to me to live is Christ, and to die is gain."[6] "Do you not know that your body is a temple of the Holy Spirit within you, whom you have from God? You are not your own, for you were bought with a price. So glorify God in your body."[7]

In Christianity, you have to die so that someone else can live through you.

The California pastor Rick Warren, best-selling author of *The Purpose Driven Life*, agrees with Paul and Jesus. He has sold tens of millions of books worldwide to worshipful believers who have been conned into thinking that life is not life. He has convinced his flock that it is actually good to be a slave. For political reasons, the fame he has achieved as a shepherd preaching sheephood got him invited to offer the opening prayer at President Barack Obama's first inauguration. What an irony that the most important civic ritual belonging to all Americans, the swearing in of our secular president, had to be "solemnized" by a superstitious sermonizer who believes that the authority of our nation stems not from we, the people, in pursuit of happiness, but from the sovereignty of a "Lord" who dictates that we must submit to his will because a talking snake tricked us into eating the fruit of knowledge. I am not going to analyze Warren's entire book; others have already done that. Robert M. Price's book, *The Reason Driven Life*, neatly exposes the fact that *The Purpose Driven Life* is nothing more than newly packaged old-fashioned biblical fundamentalism.

More than that, Warren himself has acted no better than other evangelists who pretend to have a higher calling. Before he became wealthy selling sanctimonious self-help (the "self" not being the reader), he was charged with abusing the IRS tax code. In the early 1990s, his church had paid all or a substantial part of his salary as a cash "housing allowance," allowing him to report little or no income, taking advantage of a little-known, unfair provision in the statutes that allows "ministers of the gospel" to exclude their rent or house payments from income, greatly lowering their tax liability.[8] What Warren did was clearly wrong—he was excluding his entire salary as if he were spending it all on housing. He was cheating the rest of us taxpayers. But since the law was ambiguously stated, not setting a limit to the allowance, he did not have to pay penalties or back taxes. Congress mooted the case in 2002, getting Warren off the hook, but clarifying that from now on the housing allowance is limited to the fair rental value of the home.[9] This pastor, like most clergy, apparently feels that preachers are a privileged class. His parishioners might have a purpose-driven life, but their leader has a loophole-driven life.

When Rick Warren talks about purpose, he means it only in its secondary usage. "It's not about you," he preaches. It's all about God. He believes you have no say in your own purpose. "His purpose for your life predates your conception," Warren confidently informs us, speaking about the specific deity depicted in his holy book. "He planned it before you existed, without your input! You may choose your career, your spouse, your hobbies, and many other parts of your life, but you don't get to choose your purpose."

Warren is exactly right, if you think the Christian scriptures are true. The New Testament tells Christians that they have no purpose of their own: "For to me to live is Christ, and to die is gain."[10] Jesus reportedly said: "If anyone would come after me, let him deny himself and take up his cross daily and follow me."[11]

So, what is the purpose of life, according to Rick Warren? Let me save you the trouble of reading his book by summarizing his answer: the purpose of life is to worship God, fellowship with Christians, become like Christ, serve others, and evangelize. That's it! You were born so that you can get others to join you in church. (Don't forget to put some tax-free money in the plate.) "If you want to know why you were placed on this planet," Warren assures us, "you must begin with God. You were born *by* his purpose and *for* his purpose."[12]

You are a hammer. A wrench. A pair of pliers.

Warren then insults atheists by insisting that those of us who do not hold his beliefs lead empty lives: "Without God, life has no purpose, and without purpose, life has no meaning. Without meaning, life has no significance or hope."[13] What planet is Reverend Warren living on? It seems he hasn't met many atheists. He doesn't know that hundreds of millions of good people do not "begin with God," do not believe in a god, yet live full meaningful lives. We are not the ones with the problem! We are alive. We think it is sad that so many human beings pretend to have no purpose of their own, that they are so willing to "die to themselves" (as the bible commands), submitting to someone else's plan for their lives.

If you need a purpose-driven life, you are an actor in someone else's play. You are following a script for a B-rated movie—a bible-rated movie. If your existence has meaning only while it is being directed in someone else's film, you have no life of your own. You have been robbed. We nonbelievers think you deserve better. We think you should throw away the script, make your own movie, emancipate yourself, and reclaim your rightful property and place in this world. Get a life!

In my book *The Good Atheist,* I describe how the postures of prayer are identical to the postures of slavery: knees bent, wrists shackled in humble obedience, eyes closed, head bowed, body prostrate before the master. "For you were bought at a price," said Paul the slave, "therefore glorify God in your body and in your spirit, which are God's."[14] There is indeed a purpose in this, but it is not your own. It is directed from outside your own life. "Whatever you do," Paul also wrote, "do all to the glory of God."[15] Christians are toddlers who simply do what the parent says, "bringing every thought into captivity unto the obedience of Christ."[16] (The next time someone tells you there is freedom in Christ, read that verse to them. Whatever "captivity" is, it is not freedom.) In Christianity, the ultimate purpose is to glorify and worship the master, not to live or enjoy your own life. Even good works—which you would think should be aimed at the recipients of charity—are ultimately focused on the majesty of the heavenly father: "Let your light so shine before men, that they may see your good works and glorify your Father in heaven."[17] The biblical writers were shameless about this redirection of purpose: "If I was trying to please men," Paul wrote, "I would not be a slave of Christ."[18]

According to slave traders like Rick Warren (all Christian ministers are slave traders), we are not on this plantation called earth for our own sakes. Our existence is all about glory. But what is glory, if not the puffing up of one individual above everybody else? "Thou art worthy, O Lord, to receive glory and honour and power: for thou hast created all things, and for thy pleasure they are and were created."[19] Our own pleasure is irrelevant. If one person is raised above all others, it follows that everyone else is inferior. *You* are second rate. Christianity is a huge put-down of humanity. It is the glorification of one individual who enjoys being a slave master over the powerless.

What is wrong with this picture? We normally detest a person who claims to own and control other human beings, so why do we think it is admirable when God does it? Because might makes right? Why do we honor that which we naturally despise? If you were a god, would you actually want others to bow down and kiss your feet? And what would the rest of us think of you? If there actually exists a praise-thirsty deity like the bible describes, then why should we worship him? Because he is the big boss and he demands it? Because if you don't put your hands together and tell him how great he is you will be sent down into the basement?

Is that what life is all about?

Would you rather watch a movie about loyal captive subjects in the service of their omnipotent master, or a movie about a slave revolt? Which would be more exciting? What characters would you root for and sympathize with? So, why just a movie? Why not make your own life a slave revolt?

To live freely is to escape the tyranny of a sovereign. It is to start a proud revolutionary war defying the king with a declaration of independence. When human beings are subjugated "under absolute Despotism, it is their right, it is their duty, to throw off such Government."[20]

Asking, "If there is no God, what is the purpose of life?" is like asking, "If there is no Master, whose slave will I be?" If the purpose of life is to become a submissive slave, then your meaning comes from flattering the ego of a person whom you should despise.

Fortunately, all of that is moot. You don't have to fear the basement. There is no basement. There is no master. There is no lord. You can just keep walking, and live your own life.

Here is the good news we atheists offer to the world:

There is no purpose of life.

It may sound counterintuitive, but that is truly great news! Life is its own reward. You should not want there to be a purpose of life. You are not a subject. You don't have an assignment to live up to. You don't have a cosmic task to accomplish. You don't have a duty to fulfill. You are not being managed or judged by an overlord. Unshackled from the chains of a master, you are truly free to live.

Since life is its own reward, it can't have any purpose above and beyond itself. Of course, life is survival and reproduction, but that is a definition of life, not a purpose of life. If there is a God, what is the purpose of *his* life? Does he sit up in heaven, looking around, asking, "Why am I here?"

Now, here is the point on which this whole book hinges: to say there is no purpose *of* life is not to say there is no purpose *in* life.

Life has immense purpose, not from outside, but from inside. Look what a huge difference a tiny preposition makes: purpose *of* life versus purpose *in* life.[21] Your life has purpose because it is endowed not by someone else's mind, but by your own. One is bondage; the other is liberty.

So, if there is no purpose of life, but there is purpose in life, then where does it come from? How can you find a life-driven purpose?

You don't find it. In most cases, it finds you. You create it yourself by your intention to keep living your life as fully as possible, overcoming any obstacles in your way. Since your life is in many ways different from everyone else's, those obstacles and challenges will not be exactly the same for you as for the rest of the world.

Purpose comes from solving problems. You don't look for an intention before you know what you want or need to do. You can't answer a question before it is asked. It is only *after* you identify a lack, or desire, or value, or goal, that you "head for it." The "heading for" is the purpose, the intention in action. I think it is the very struggle to solve problems that makes life what it is. It makes life exciting!

Life is not driven by purpose; purpose is driven by life. You don't have a purpose-driven life; you have life-driven purpose.

If you are still religious and are struggling with "what it all means," then here is a purpose: get rid of the problem. Start a slave rebellion. Depose the dictator. Live your own life.

In my books *Losing Faith in Faith* and *Godless,* I tell the story of how I went from evangelical preacher to atheist. It is not my task here to explain why I and millions of other good people do not believe in a god or an afterlife. I describe it all in great detail in those books. My point here is to show that whatever you think about the conclusions of atheists, you can't claim that we lead empty, meaningless lives.

I used to think I had a life of purpose when I was spreading the Gospel and "glorifying God," but I now see that was a cheap substitute for life. Since the real world is the only world that matters, preaching a nonexistent fantasy world is a huge waste of time. In *Godless,* I make the case that if I was not a true Christian, nobody is. I believed it all, utterly and completely. I dedicated my life to the service of my imaginary lord Jesus. I now see how thin and artificial the pretense was. Imagining that doing nothing is actually meaningful, I gained immense unearned respect from congregants who desperately wanted someone else to tell them how to live, how to think, how to find the purpose of their lives. There would be no shepherds without sheep. Like Rick Warren, I found a "calling," a "purpose-driven life," due to the fact that so many people think purpose must come from outside themselves. My life of ministry was possible only as the result of this primitive, cowering mind-set of sheep wanting a shepherd.

It wasn't until I got out of the master-slave ministry that I learned what real purpose is. Real purpose comes from solving real problems, not phony problems like "how can I be saved?" When I knew I would be leaving the ministry, after nineteen years of preaching, I had a concrete problem. I needed a job. I often hear from other clergy with the same dilemma: they have happily jettisoned their faith, but what do they do now? They spent years doing nothing of any real purpose: preaching, teaching, organizing worship, counseling parishioners, evangelizing, missionizing. What good are they now that they no longer believe? Who are they? How easy will it be for them to get a new job when all they have is a divinity degree? As I wrote in *Godless*, some of them end up in education, such as teaching philosophy, or go into social work, which are fields commensurate with their experience. Some go into sales—a different kind of evangelism. Some start their own business. But people are not cats: it is not easy to land on your feet when you have been turned upside down.[22]

Let me tell you a story about how I found life-driven purpose in the real world after leaving the ministry. In 1983, the same year I told myself I was an atheist and needed to stop preaching, I took an Introduction to Computer Programming class at Chaffey College. It was very basic: well, we learned the BASIC programming language. I entered my first algorithms on punch cards. Before the class was over I landed a job! (I never got a degree in computer science or even took another programming class.) My uncle Keith had an industrial software company and he offered me an entry-level position, not as a programmer, but as an assistant entering data for the programmers. I loved it! We were building a monitoring system for tank farms—mostly petroleum, but it could be any liquid—creating a real-time multitasking system in 68000 Assembly Language from the ground up. I had to move from BASIC down to a low-level language that was closer to the machine, riskier but fun. It was like driving stick shift instead of automatic.

For some reason the contract was put on hold for six months, but Keith decided to keep us on the payroll so that we could hit the ground running when the work started up again. For half a year, I did little else but read manuals and talk to programmers. Keith decided to test my talents, so he tossed me a couple of simple programs. The first one I wrote was the trivial function to convert between Fahrenheit and Centigrade (we were truly building from scratch), and I tackled it as if it were the most crucial assignment on earth. After he approved my code and added it to the system, I remember driving home that day, thinking, "I'm a programmer!" I was being paid to do one of the funnest things in the world. But most important, I didn't have to preach any more. Solving a real problem was much more meaningful than saving fictional souls from a fictional hell.

During those months, we were allowed to put in 40 hours a week any way we wanted, so I often worked 10–12 hours a day, leaving me long weekends to continue running down my calendar of preaching engagements. Those were the hypocritical weeks I write about in *Godless* when I was still preaching but not believing a word of it, finally ending about five months later with that dramatic December event in Auburn, California, where I broke it off for good. "That's it. I'm outa here." It was like growing up and leaving home all over again,[23] though this time I was actually glad to get out of the house. I could leave the ministry because I had a job, a way out, a purpose-filled life.

During those six months on hold, I had practically memorized the 68000 manual. My work was on the user interface, so I had to know what everyone else was doing. I had to see the big picture. Evangelism—inviting people to become servants—was a small picture. I never knew a real job could be such a blast.

That project ended in about a year, so I needed another job. I heard that Safetran, a company that builds dispatching systems for the railroads, was hiring programmers. I drove to Cucamonga for the first real job interview in my life. (I didn't have to interview for any of my earlier pastoral positions. I was invited to those churches, and all I had to do was accept.) I had limited experience and no degree in computers—I didn't mention I had been a preacher—but the manager was impressed that I had programmed in assembly language. When he asked me that awkward "tell me about yourself" question, I replied, "There's nothing I can't do," exaggerating a lot. "Give me a problem, and I will solve it." He must have liked that attitude, because I got the job.

I quickly found I was in *way* over my head, but they never knew it. I learned the Pascal language and looked over the shoulders of the veterans, trying not to look stupid. I took manuals home, toiled late into the night and came into work early. At first I was behind, but it didn't matter. Every week during the progress meeting I noticed there was always someone else struggling to get through the bottleneck ahead of my task, so when they asked me how I was doing, I always said, "I'm right on schedule." By the time it mattered, I was. One day, they announced that Norfolk-Southern was requesting a new feature for a dispatching system in the Midwest, and I volunteered to write it. It was the cascade task that allows dispatchers to set a route by moving switches and hit a single key that clears a train through multiple locations. This interfaced with all of the other tasks, so again I had to see the big picture.

There were *huge* problems to solve, but I loved it. "I get paid to do this?!" It was like playing with a train set, except the trains were real. (Later, when I was working in Galesburg, Illinois, a worker was killed and another lost a leg when they forgot to spike their switch and a car at the hump yard rolled over them. They tried to blame our software, but the federal safety investigation proved it was a combination of dispatcher error and worker sloppiness. It was indeed serious business.) When it was time to install the system in Fort Wayne, they asked if any of us could go to Indiana for six to nine months to set it up and test it. I volunteered. The forty-foot semicircular display was already in place, showing the signals, gates, switches, and snow melters for the railroad system in northern Indiana and parts of Ohio, Michigan, and Illinois.

When we California programmers walked into that Indiana dispatching center, we were met with scowls. The huge, windowless, smoke-filled room was inhabited by large men wearing beards and overalls, some chewing tobacco. The labor union was upset that our newfangled computers were putting people out of work. Some even cursed at us softy West Coast liberals, telling us they hoped our contraption would fail. (Strangely, I was enjoying the new feeling of being called a liberal.) Whenever something went wrong, they would snicker and spit. Some of those men liked to hang out at "lingerie parties" after work. I quickly discovered that the only thing Fort Wayne had more of than churches was strip joints, and I was sure they were in cahoots. There would be little Sunday confessing without Saturday "sinning." When my preacher-to-atheist story became known, I became a target of some of those upstanding hypocritical role models who thought I was the one who needed moral advice.

One day I took a walk along the tracks during lunch break and noticed some little purple and yellow flowers that had volunteered to grow by a pile of railroad ties. I brought some inside and put them in a coffee mug beside my terminal. After a while one of the dispatchers hesitated as he walked by.

"You brought flowers in here?" he asked. The room became quiet.

"They're pretty," I said. "They add some color to this drab place."

"You aren't gay, are you?" Someone else laughed.

I stared at the big guy. "Do you have to be gay to appreciate beauty? No, I'm not gay, but what if I were? There are probably some gay people here at this station." He looked around the room.

"About one person in ten is homosexual," I continued. "The odds are that you have a gay coworker and don't know it."

He looked around and said, "Well, there are only nine people in this room." At that moment their supervisor walked in and someone yelled, "There's the tenth person!" We all laughed. So did the supervisor, eventually.

I never preached about homosexuality during my entire ministry. We were all sinners, I believed, so why single out any group? But now, suddenly, it did matter. I had something important to say, and it wasn't about insulting the "holiness" of a god by "choosing" a lifestyle that is forbidden by the bible. It was about offending humanity. God may be a delusion but the intolerance and harm that comes from faith is real. Religious discrimination is something actually worth preaching against and the lack of fairness is a noble problem to tackle. Fighting prejudice is one way to have a purpose-filled life.

If purpose comes from solving problems, I had plenty of it on that job. There was one intermittent and elusive bug on that project that seemed utterly intractable. A certain software flag was sometimes not being reset when the server task finished its job, resulting in an incorrect display and a sluggishness in the system that had to be corrected by hand. It was potentially dangerous and totally unacceptable. We wrestled with that bug for almost a month. We discussed it during midnight meals. The client was getting impatient and angry, and so were our managers. We tried all kinds of kluge solutions, ugly band-aid fixes that not only added layers of inelegant code, but slowed it down, and didn't work anyway. They flew in a high-priced consultant from California, a small man with a bow tie and black briefcase who entered the hopeful room as if he were the God of Technology. The first thing he did was spill coffee on one of the custom terminals, shorting it out, making us wait until a new one could be flown in overnight from Los Angeles. A lot of very smart people were losing sleep over this emergency.

I love that state of uncertainty when you know you have a problem that can be solved but you haven't got there yet. I had felt that way when I was struggling with the question of the existence of God. I didn't give up. "Something is wrong, and I can figure this out," I often repeated. The brain goes full-speed ahead attacking the problem, then it backs off, looks around, combs the memory banks for similar or parallel situations. It gets ravenous for data, scavenging for clues. "Don't give up, don't give up. There is something to learn here." After running out of ideas, you put it aside, sleep on it, try to sneak up on it laterally. During times like that, life definitely has purpose.

And then I got it. Sitting at my terminal by the little flowers, surrounded by experts, degreed programmers, analysts, dispatchers in overalls, managers, and big bosses in suits who were arguing about the blame, it came to me in a flash. I saw a solution that seemed so obvious that when the other programmers later heard of it they all said, "I could have thought of that!" (They could have, but they didn't.) I got the solution by thinking heretically. Up to that point, failing to spot an error in the code or locate some flaky hardware, we were trying to fix the problem by adding complexity. We were forced to work around the quirky problem in the server task, but the radical unthinkable question came into my mind: do we even need the server task? No one had even considered that. It was like asking if we can live without a kidney. Or a god. Yes, you can, it turns out. You can sometimes solve a problem by simply removing it.

The server task was like a butler, handing data to the other tasks. All the switches, tracks, sidings, signals, gates—everything that constitutes a railroad location—were in a huge bunch of tables in the database. The purpose of the server task was to fetch that data for other tasks. It was designed to be flexible. Some stations were more complex than others, and to keep each of the tasks free from such drudge work, the server acted as a gofer. When it finished its job, it set a flag to say it was free, like the light on the top of a New York City taxi. Except the flag sometimes did not get reset, and that was the problem.

Seeing the big picture, it dawned on me that in the Fort Wayne system there was only one other task that was actually requesting the data. I realized that if the database were small enough to fit within the code space of the requesting task, it could simply be moved into a local array, and the server would not be needed. (This was before the days of relational databases and virtually unlimited memory.) I was disappointed at first, because the data turned out to be too large—but just by a little bit! Not giving up, I realized I could tighten up the code in the invoking task, making it take up less space though run a bit slower. I knew that this loss of speed would be more than compensated for by not having to wait for the server task. (My solution was not ideal in general, but I was sure it would work for Fort Wayne.)

I walked over to my manager, who was standing by his boss, and told him what I had in mind. He crossed his eyes and looked at me like,

"Are you crazy?!" The specs did not call for such a radical nephrectomy. What else might be affected? The law of unintended consequences is very strong in software systems. Trains were moving! What if my "fix" made things worse? I agreed that the queue of commands would back up if it didn't work, but assured him that I could quickly replace the old task and drain the queue to catch up with real time. So he swallowed hard and announced to the group: "I want to try something." He nodded at me. I had already tested the code in a fake environment, so I quickly pasted it into the task, all while trains were running. It was like performing heart surgery on a racer who is approaching the finish line. I installed the update and then looked anxiously up at the board showing the trains in motion.

It was quiet for a moment, then one of the dispatchers said, "What happened?" The problem went away! The bug disappeared and the system was faster. Cheers and high fives! When we later removed the kluges, it ran even better. We never did figure out what was wrong, and no longer needed to. The credit went to the team, as it should have—my manager was promoted a few weeks later—but among the programmers I was a hero for a day, until the next problem came along.

Solving that problem, even just striving to solve it, gave me purpose in life. It felt like I was . . . alive.

As the server task problem showed, sometimes simplicity is better than complexity. A universe with a god is more complicated than one without it. In order to fix all the bugs in the God task—the absence of evidence, the problem of evil, the lack of agreement among believers, the lack of a coherent definition, the uncertainty of the interpretation of unreliable holy books, the oppression of women and minorities and heretics, the failure of prayer (flag not being reset?), the dangers of sectarian divisiveness, and so on—believers need to cobble together inelegant Rube Goldberg kluges, apologetics, theologies, and theodicies to keep it clunking along. But if we can excise the God task and simply say, "No thanks, I'll handle it myself," things will run much more smoothly. A radical faithectomy can work wonders on a sick system.

We don't need a God task to hand us our purpose. If you think purpose comes from a holy messenger who hands you a platter with a note saying, "Do this," what happens when the communication breaks down? What happens when your requests are ignored? What happens when you realize that the scripture is a corrupted database? What if the messenger gets sick or dies? What do you do when you learn your religious leaders have been lying to you and your "master" is just a fiction? Is your life wasted? Are you nothing? Are you just a Frankenstein monster needing an outside spark to make you move? Or are you an evolved human being with an intelligent mind full of ideas, instincts, values, plans, and purposes of your own? Like I did with the server task, move your purpose from outside to inside.

Rick Warren is not the only Christian author who thinks we need to search for purpose outside of ourselves. Televangelist Joel Osteen, pastor of the huge Lakewood Church in Houston, puts down the human race with similar words: "God is in control and he has a great plan and purpose for your life. Your dreams may not have turned out exactly as you'd hoped, but the bible says that God's ways are better and higher than our ways."[24] This simplistic rah-rah "just trust God" inspirational writing is supposed to make believers feel better, not by offering any practical advice, but simply by saying the words they want to hear. No matter what happens in life, somehow, God's "purpose" (whatever that is) will magically occur. Isn't that wonderful?

Compared to unsophisticated preachers like Warren and Osteen, the philosopher and Christian apologist Dr. William Lane Craig is much more informed and articulate, but he is just as wrong. In his book *Reasonable Faith*, Craig claims that if purpose is not "ultimate," it is worthless. "If each person passes out of existence when he dies," he asks, "then what ultimate meaning can be given to his life?" He replies with the nonsequitur, "Thus, if there is no God, then life itself becomes meaningless. Man and the universe are without ultimate significance." How does it follow that if there is no "ultimate significance," life is meaningless? Craig doesn't make the connection. He seems to be confusing meaning with "ultimate meaning" (whatever that is). He thinks we are hammers. This is very much like Rick Warren conflating the two different usages of purpose.

Purpose and meaning scurry through Craig's book like greased piglets. He never defines purpose (as I do) or meaning (as I will in the final chapter). He sloppily treats them as synonyms. Neither does he directly define absurd: "For if there is no God, then man's life becomes absurd." What does absurd mean? "It means that the life we have is without ultimate significance, value, or purpose."[25] So life is absurd if there is no ultimate meaning, but life lacks meaning because without God it is absurd. He is talking in a circle. According to believers like Craig who are unhappy with blunt reality, life needs to be more than it is, otherwise it is absurd, and since we can't possibly allow life to be absurd, then life must be more than it is! As an atheist, I think *that* is absurd.

He also confuses ultimate with objective. "Without God, there can be no objective meaning of life," Craig writes. "In order to be happy, one must believe in objective meaning, value, and purpose." But he doesn't connect the dots. He pulls "objective" like a rabbit out of a hat, as if the existence of an unproved supernatural being could be remotely objective or have any logical connection to purpose. (If there is a God, what is *his* ultimate objective purpose?)

"If God does not exist," he continues, "then you are just a miscarriage of nature, thrust into a purposeless universe to live a purposeless life." If we don't believe in God, "all we are left with is despair." Craig, being religiously colorblind (see chapter 3) and unable to imagine what motivates abolitionists, seems not to realize that most atheists indeed live rich lives of value, meaning, and purpose that is grounded in objective reality. He shows that he does not grasp the difference between purpose *of* life and purpose *in* life: "Only if God exists can there be purpose in life." That is simply sophomoric, a miscarriage of reason. Whether God exists or not, there is purpose in life.

Suppose you have been working hard at your job and are excitedly looking forward to an earned vacation in a few weeks. It will be a fun and refreshing break. Perhaps you are planning to ski, swim, hike, explore, travel, or visit friends or relatives. But then you realize, "Oh! When it's over I'll have to come back to work!" Would you cancel your vacation because it won't last forever and has no "ultimate meaning"?

Craig creates a false dichotomy: "It seems to me positively irrational to prefer death, futility, and destruction to life, meaningfulness, and happiness. As Pascal said, we have nothing to lose and infinity to gain." Does he really imagine we atheists *prefer* death, futility, and destruction? Does he seriously think that even if the universe is ultimately purposeless we nonbelievers are not leading meaningful and happy lives while we are on this planet?

"Only here, in intimate communion with one's Creator, does man find authentic existence." There's another phrase Craig fails to define. If you exist, aren't you authentic? Claiming that atheists have "inauthentic existence" is like labeling someone an "illegitimate child," and we know what the word for that is. "Authentic existence" apparently means "believing in God," though the connection is not clear. Is eternal more authentic than temporal? Is longer more authentic than shorter? Is credulity more authentic than skepticism, or faith more authentic than doubt? Are Christians the only real humans? Are the rest of us artificial and cheap? If a serious philosopher is going to make such claims, he should explain and defend them.

Craig's only explanation is to preach: "This is the horror of modern man: because he ends in nothing, he is nothing." I have rarely read a more pathetic sentence. Does Craig really think that anything short of eternal is nothing? My life of learning, loving, parenting, helping, and enjoyment counts for nothing? Our entire lives of purpose, productivity, and morality are just a "horror"? Speak for yourself, Dr. Craig.

The preachers have got it completely backward. If life is eternal, then life is cheap. Value does not come from surplus; it comes from rarity. Prices rise as supply drops. The reality that our lives are brief is what makes them precious. The fact that they will end makes them *more* meaningful. "Ultimate purpose" is no purpose at all: it is the surrender of purpose. It is the pretense that faith equals meaning.

Peter Hitchens, the believing Anglican brother of the late Christopher Hitchens, believes like William Lane Craig that there is something wrong with the attitudes and personal choices of atheists, creating the same false dichotomy. In November 2012, I participated in a debate in Oxford, England, put on by the prestigious Oxford Union Society.[26] The famous skeptic and author Michael Shermer, philosopher Peter Millican, and I teamed up against mathematician John Lennox, Anglican priest Joanna Collicut, and Peter Hitchens. It was formal wear—tuxedos and black ties—in parliamentarian format. The proposition was "This house believes in God." After Shermer and I made our statements, Hitchens took the floor. He immediately admitted he had no proof or evidence for God, but then turned to us atheists (Richard Dawkins was sitting right behind us) and continued with an outrageous ad hominem accusation:

> The real question before us is why we choose what we choose. . . . Why would you want to live in a purposeless chaos, in which none of your actions had any significance, in which there was no hope of justice, in which the lives of all those whom you loved ended abruptly at death and had no further significance. Why would you want, desire, actively wish to live in a universe as disgusting as that? You have to have a very good reason. And I think these gentlemen do have a

very good reason, and it's what they never ever wish to discuss. They *don't* want justice. They *do* want the dead to be dead. They *do* want the universe to be purposeless. They do not want their individual actions to have any other significance than their immediate effect. You'll have to discuss with them why they should be so keen on that proposition.

There was no time for me to make a rebuttal that evening. (I wish I could have asked Peter Hitchens if he thinks his brother is in hell.) But if he is reading this, let me reply. We atheists do want justice. Why would you imagine we don't? As with purpose, justice doesn't have to be ultimate to be meaningful. We want justice in *our* world, not in a pretend supernatural realm. Since there is no ultimate cosmic justice, we have all the *more* reason not to put it off to an uncertain future. We had better do it now. We atheists *do* want our loved ones to live on, but we are honest and courageous enough to admit that our personal desires do not alter the reality of death. We atheists *do* want purpose in the universe, and in fact we do have it, in our personal lives, not in an empty cosmic "purpose of life" for which you admit there is no evidence. We atheists *do* want our actions to have more than their immediate effect—not an irrelevant cosmic effect, but a long-lasting effect in the world where we live. In his book, *What I Believe,* Bertrand Russell wrote:

> I believe that when I die I shall rot, and nothing of my ego will survive. I am not young and I love life. But I should scorn to shiver with terror at the thought of annihilation. Happiness is nonetheless true happiness because it must come to an end, nor do thought and love lose their value because they are not everlasting. Many a man has borne himself proudly on the scaffold; surely the same pride should teach us to think truly about man's place in the world. Even if the open windows of science at first make us shiver after the cosy indoor warmth of traditional humanizing myths, in the end the fresh air brings vigour, and the great spaces have a splendour of their own.

Just as Russell said, "Happiness is nonetheless true happiness because it must come to an end," I think we can say the same thing about purpose.

Since purpose comes from solving problems, and since problems are material, it follows that purpose can only deal with the natural world. "Spiritual purpose" is an oxymoron, and if it isn't, it is still irrelevant. The word "spirit" has never been defined, so it can't describe a purpose or anything else. (More about this in chapter 4.)

By the way, Christians believe that when they get to heaven there will be no more struggle, pain, or sorrow. This means there will be no problems to solve during an eternity of praising the Master. Since purpose comes from solving problems, heaven will be Ultimate Purposelessness!

Most believers think the mere material world can't have purpose. Our lives must be directed from outside in order to have meaning, they preach. They imagine that the spiritual, whatever it is, is superior to the natural. They view the natural world as low and debased, while the supernatural is lofty and sublime.

It is not just believers from the Abrahamic tradition who feel this way. I have done many debates with Christians, Jews, and Islamic scholars, but I recently did my first debate with a Hindu, in Toronto. His name is Shankara Baghavadpada, a former physicist from the city of Chennai in India's southern state of Tamil Nadu. He is very friendly, gentle, and kind. We shook hands and hugged. We truly like each other as human beings. He calls himself a Vedic astrologer, although there is no Hindu astrology (Jyotisha) in the Vedas. He writes that Hindu civilization has been compromised, and he is certainly right about that. English-educated Indians, he claims, have lost sight of their true nature. The world has been infected with a malady that makes us blind to spiritual reality and deaf to the voice of Shiva. "In India, the quest for God is a life-time journey," Shankara says. "You don't do this as a summer crash course." It is only with great difficulty and dedication that some masters over the age of sixty (like himself), under the skillful tutelage of earlier masters, have been able to take the long journey approaching the state of *moksha* where the self is completely obliterated and can glimpse the true reality that we are more than just "puny biophysical organisms." Those who are unenlightened, however, can touch this reality by seeking advice from the masters, who will interpret our horoscope charts professionally (for a fee). A Vedic astrologer, knowing your exact moment of birth, claims to be able to discern meaning from the positions of the planets in the zodiac and can tell you whether you should start a business, get married to a particular person, get married on a certain date, begin a family sooner or later, and so on. Vedic astrologers insist they can predict a person's intelligence just by knowing their birthday.

All of this has been disproved scientifically. In addition to hundreds of studies in the West, there was also a careful experiment conducted in India. Professor Narlikar at the University of Pune enlisted twenty-seven eager, experienced Vedic astrologers to test their predictive powers in a careful double-blind experiment. The results of that study showed that you can achieve the same success with a coin toss.[27]

After telling the audience at that Toronto debate that I am also an Indian—I am a Lenni Lenape, a Delaware Indian, and my tribal name is Sook Kah-lon Ah-hos, which means "Rain Crow"—I pretended to channel the spirit of one of my ancient ancestors:

Shankara, I have a message for you. I am Sook Kah-lon Ah-hos, the timeless Lenape spirit. I lived in the flesh on the American continent almost fifteen thousand years ago, many millennia before your Hindu civilization existed. I am the person who created Shiva. I also created Odin for the north, Quetzalcoatl for the Aztecs, Zeus for the Greeks, Yahweh for the Jews, Ishtar for the Babylonians, Venus for the Romans, and thousands of gods around the world, including Vishnu, Brahma, and the elephant god Ganesha for the Indian Subcontinent where you live. I created Shiva so that you can be guided out of the error and healed of the illness that has infected our species. Shiva is indeed leading you to the perfect state of moksha, to the top of the mountain where you will lose your self and find full enlightenment.

But what you don't know, what Hindu civilization has never known, and what Shiva himself does not know, is that moksha is not the end of the journey. It is only the first half, Shankara. When you get to the peak, to the summit of total self-abnegation, you will finally reach the vantage point to see that there is another side of the mountain. A mountain peak is great to visit, but you can't live there. It is cold and inhospitable. You have to come down the other side, where you eventually get to the bottom where you live your real life to rediscover your true nature. You will learn that the ultimate reality that you have experienced your entire life but have been unable or unwilling to see is this:

You are an animal.

We are all animals. We are indeed, as you write, puny biophysical organisms, and that is enough. It is more than enough. It is wonderful. It is the reality of who we truly are.

When you come back down the mountain, you will arrive at the state before you became sick, and stop denying your true human nature. You will no longer need to pretend that we exist in a supernatural plane. You will abandon the delusion that we are transcendent beings and rejoin the human race, proudly affirming the awesome fact that we are living material beings. We are not spirits. We are not souls. We are animals.

The journey you are taking, Shankara, is only necessary because, as you write, society is sick. Jesus admitted the same thing when he said those who are healthy don't need a doctor. And who are the healthy ones? Nonbelievers. Atheists don't need to make the journey at all. They don't have to go up and over the mountain to be cured. They are already at the ground level of reality.

You are right to point out that the human race is sick. The illness that has tormented the world is religion. All over the planet—on my continent, in Africa, on the Indian Subcontinent, in South America, Asia, Southeast Asia, Europe, everywhere—our species has been infected with faith. And you will be cured of that malady, Shankara, when you do finally see over the summit, beyond the glass darkly, past the illusion, to gain the wisdom and courage to acknowledge the face-to-face truth that has been blocked by the mountainous virus of religion. Your eyes will open to the humble but glorious truth that we are nothing more than puny physical organisms.

You will be healed of religion.

Since I created the gods—since we human animals created the gods—we can simply uncreate them. We don't need to be born again. We merely have to recognize and embrace who we were when we were first born.

I then asked Shankara if he believed that I was really channeling a dead ancestor. He shook his head "No." I congratulated him for his skepticism, for his ability to think critically and to reject obviously deluded claims. I reminded him that this is exactly what I have done with *his* claims. I don't know if he grasped this point, but that is not what bothered him. He was most upset with being called—gasp!—a physical organism. "No, we are not animals," he insisted, as if I had just insulted him. "I am a bundle of light." He thinks we are spiritual beings. When I pointed to our bodies and reminded him that there is nothing special about us, that we share molecules, genes, proteins, and instincts with all other creatures, he said, "Yes, but we are not just animals."

"But when you say we are not *just* animals," I countered, "you are admitting that we are *at least* animals." Shankara and I agree that we are "puny biophysical organisms," but he thinks we are also something above and beyond our physical existence. Just like the apostle Paul, Shankara says, "The body is just an outer covering which is cast off and dead." And that is what the whole theistic debate is about. Transcendence. My point is that we should not deny who we actually are, no matter what we think about what else we might be. If you believe we are animals *plus*, that does not mean you think we are not animals. It means you would be ashamed to consider yourself *merely* an animal.

Transcendence doesn't elevate us. It puts us down.

Being called an animal is not an insult. It is a compliment. We are very smart animals. We live our lives, our real lives, our only lives, in a physical world, the only world we know about. I don't think there is another world—I am convinced there isn't—but even if there were some metaphysical or transcendent sphere (yet to be discovered), it is irrelevant. Purpose comes from solving material problems in the material world, real problems in the real world.

And even if you disagree—if you believe there are spirits, deities, demons, and holy ghosts struggling for your soul in a supernatural realm—it does not follow that we atheists lack purpose as we live our biophysical lives in the only world we acknowledge to exist. As long as physical problems exist, there is ample opportunity for a life of purpose.

Does a raven ask itself, "What is the purpose of my life?" as it finds creative ways to obtain food? Do cats struggle with existential anxiety? Do pandas ask, "Why am I here?" I have read that elephants grieve, but do they wonder what happens after they die? Don't they just live? Why can't life be awesome on its own? Life is short and often difficult, but why cheapen it? Are we so insecure and unhappy that we must denigrate ourselves in order for life to "make sense"? Why can't we human animals do like the others and simply live without pretense?

Religion is a refusal to face reality. It teaches us to be ashamed of who we are. It turns the head away in disappointment. In the mythical story of Adam and Eve, I don't think eating from the tree of knowledge was a crime—the crime was seeing ourselves for who we really are and being ashamed: "And the eyes of them both were opened, and they knew that they were naked; and they sewed fig leaves together, and made themselves aprons."[28] Religion is the apron, a mask to cover our true natures. It teaches us to distrust our own purposes.

We atheists are not ashamed of our human nature, our lives, our purposes. In *The Good Atheist*, I profiled hundreds of atheists and non-believers who have lived purposeful lives. Elizabeth Cady Stanton working for universal suffrage—the radical idea that women can participate in their own democracy—Margaret Sanger struggling for birth control, W. E. B. Du Bois working for civil rights, Bill Gates combating poverty and poor health, Joe Hill organizing unions, Beatrice and Sydney Webb reforming health care. Actors, artists, authors, composers, feminists, human rights activists, journalists, playwrights, philanthropists, philosophers, poets, political leaders, psychologists, psychiatrists, reformers, revolutionaries, scientists, and songwriters.[29] The world has been richly blessed by the actions of nontheists who have cared enough about this world, the only world we are certain of, to try to meet the challenges that threaten our survival and well-being. No one can deny that these people have life-driven purpose.

Do you want a purpose-filled life? Then find a problem to solve. Usually you don't need to find a problem. It finds you. Perhaps your sibling or parent dies of a horrible illness, and you dedicate the rest of your life to fighting that disease. Maybe you see your gay friends bullied at school and you get angry enough to fight bigotry. Or maybe you are gay yourself and won't settle for being treated as a second-class citizen. Perhaps you possess a driving thirst for knowledge, or a heightened sense of wonder and awe at the unsolved mysteries of science, or a natural outrage against violence. Identify something you hate and work against it. Hunger, thirst, unsafe drinking water, natural disasters, inequality, oppression, unfairness, voter suppression, predation, disease, invasions, aggression, racism, sexism, spousal abuse, the abuse of children (sometimes by clergy), crime, cruelty to animals, homelessness, pollution, environmental degradation, species decimation, political corruption, corporate greed, unsafe working conditions, exploitation, overpopulation, theocratic persecution—these are all worth fighting.

Or find something you love and work for it. Problem solving can be positive as well as negative. Parenting, education, science, history, beauty, art, music, literature, poetry, theater, architecture, entertainment, cooking, gardening—these are all useful and purpose-filled activities, and you can certainly think of more. They are not "ultimate." They are real. Surmounting the challenges that arise in these endeavors helps to protect and enrich our existence. It gives life meaning.

I am copresident, with Annie Laurie Gaylor (we are married), of the Freedom From Religion Foundation, which has been working since 1976 to keep state and church separate. Our five full-time attorneys field literally thousands of complaints each year from people around the country who notice that our secular government, based on a godless constitution, is improperly advancing religion. We write letters of complaint and take lawsuits to correct those abuses. People sometimes ask why we bother, and we usually reply, "Is there anything more important than defending the First Amendment?" Annie Laurie has spent her entire life working for women's rights and a secular government, and who would dare claim that her life lacks purpose?

I know I am running the risk of sounding motivational, even preachy. (What do you expect of a former pastor?) Most atheists don't need or want someone to tell them what to think, and I am certainly not pretending to be a Deacon of Atheism or Bishop of Freethought. We all think our own thoughts, bottom-up, not from a top-down authority. Atheism is a movement with no followers. We are all leaders. But this book is aimed at countering sermonizers like Rick Warren and William Lane Craig who are not telling the truth when they preach that we nonbelievers lead vacant, purposeless lives.

The good news of atheism is that there is no purpose of life. There is purpose *in* life. Purpose does not come from magnifying the glory of a master, whether natural or supernatural. It comes from striving to make a better place of this world, the real world, the only world we have.

2

MERE MORALITY

I was in the Detroit airport when I saw the baby fall. Heading to New York City to be a guest on the *Phil Donahue Show* in 1989, I was standing in line waiting for my connecting flight to board. I was probably thinking about what I wanted to say on the show the next morning—the topic was life after death—and was not paying much attention to my surroundings. Another group was waiting to board at the next gate, and I may have noticed the young couple in that line. They had placed a baby carrier on top of a luggage cart, about three or four feet off the ground, and the father must have stepped away for a moment.

The corner of my eye saw the baby kick, my leg made a quick stride to the left, and my finger tips caught the edge of the carrier as it was rolling toward the hard floor. About a second later the mother grabbed the other side. She would have been too late. "That was scary!" I said. Neither of us wanted to let go for a few seconds, but I finally realized I should give the baby back to its mother. She took the child out of the carrier and held it close.

You should have seen the look she gave her husband.

A couple of minutes later their group boarded the plane. As they were disappearing into the jet bridge, the mother with baby in arms turned and briefly glanced at me with no expression, a quick look that I took to mean, "Thank you." That baby has probably graduated from college now, and I can imagine the story that mother might have told her child about the angel in the airport. They didn't know the angel was an atheist.

What I did was not special. You would have done the same thing. Who wants to see a baby fall to a hard floor? Few people would be able to resist acting in such a situation. I surprised myself. It was instinctive and automatic, with no conscious deliberation, as if I were watching someone else. It was immediate emotion. As I was holding onto that carrier, I felt a huge relief, as if I had just saved my own child. My body was on full alert; my breathing and heart rate sped up.

Why did I do it? I didn't know those people. We might not have liked each other. Should it matter to me if someone else's child gets hurt? Was it reciprocal altruism? Did I say to the mother, "Okay, lady, I did you a favor, now you owe me one"? Before acting, was I calculating the risk and the payback, the cost and the benefit? Did I analyze the relative merits of the consequences of acting versus not acting, or consider that I might get sued if I erred and contributed to the injury? None of that went through my mind. There was no time for analysis. What happened was an immediate, apparently subconscious impulse to act. If there was any decision to be made, it would have been whether *not* to act. It was truly a split-second reaction.

Before the baby kicked, I had not been standing there contemplating Jesus, Yahweh, Muhammad or Joseph Smith. I was not thinking, "What can I do today to bring glory to God?" or "How can I be a moral person?" or "How can I show the world that atheists are good people?" The action was beneath the level of rational moral judgment. It was biological.

We are animals, after all. We come prepackaged with an array of instincts inherited from our ancestors who were able to survive long enough to allow their genes—or closely related genes—to be passed to the next generation *because* they had those tendencies. An individual who does not care about falling babies is less likely to have his or her genes copied into the future.

Suppose instead of acting, I had dropped to my knees and prayed with a loud voice: "Dear God, help that baby!" What good would that have done? Faith is irrelevant to morality. Prayer might give believers the illusion they are doing something meaningful, but it is no more effective than random chance. Prayer is inaction. Believing in God is not the way to be good.

How do atheists know how to be good? How does anybody know how to be good? Should you simply "give a little whistle, and always let your conscience be your guide," as Jiminy Cricket counseled Pinocchio?[1] Conscience is defined as a "moral sense," but what is that, exactly? Is it a physical sense? Do we simply perceive the right thing to do? If so, why do so many people do the wrong thing, and why is it often so hard to know what is right? If our "conscience" is so dependable, why do we need laws? Why do we have moral dilemmas? Jiminy Cricket had a sweet idea but it sounds simplistic, like something you would hear in a movie. How exactly does a "conscience" guide us, and why does it not always work very well in reality? Luckily we are not puppets-turned-human or we would all have very long noses.

Should we follow a code instead? Is morality a lookup list of prescribed rules? Can it be reduced to obeying orders? Should you "always let your bible be your guide"? If so, why do believers disagree about moral issues, and why do so many of them act immorally?

C. S. Lewis tried to define a "mere Christianity," a core set of beliefs that remain after all the nonessential doctrines are stripped away.[2] In its place, I propose Mere Morality, a ground-level understanding of what it means to be good. A well-rounded life will involve much more than the moral minimum, of course, and each of us can choose how far to go beyond that, but I would like to suggest Mere Morality as the starting point. It is a C, a passing grade, a driver's permit. Mere Morality is what allows all of us, believers or not, to get out of the classroom and start living a grownup life out in the real world where the hard moral lessons are to be learned.

Mere Morality is a model, a framework that can help us visualize what we are doing when we make moral choices. Have you ever seen one of those cartoons where the character is trying to make a decision with a devil on one shoulder and an angel on the other? We often find ourselves torn between what we want to do and what we feel we should do. Since there are no angels or devils, I suggest we replace the image of those silly supernatural symbols of "good and evil" with something else. Instead of cartoon characters competing for your attention, picture instinct on one shoulder, law on the other, and reason in the middle. These make up your three "moral minds," and none of them, by itself, tells you what to do. None of them is good or bad. *Actions* are what we judge to be good or bad, and your moral minds are guides that help you do the judging.

Of course, you don't really have three separate minds; there are not three little people fighting for attention in your brain. Just like the Feynman diagrams are not intended to represent what is actually happening in quantum physics—they are a way to visually "stand for" the effects—the three minds of Mere Morality are a way to help think through moral decisions. Daniel Dennett might call this an "intuition pump,"[3] a tool for critical thinking. Your own mind is certainly multilayered, with levels of perceptual, emotional, and cognitive activities (as the story of the falling baby shows), with hundreds of separate simultaneous functions operating as modules, or "minds" within your brain above and below the level of consciousness. Emotion, for example, is more primitive than reason, and much stronger, but taking all of the different parts as a whole, we can talk about the aggregate as your one individual mind composed of separate smaller "minds."

Mere Morality considers the mind of reason to be the head on the shoulders, with instinct on one side and law on the other. Instinct and law are the results of minds. Instinct is the biological outcome of decisions made by the minds of your ancestors, and law is the result of the collective decisions made by the many minds of the social group in which you live. Law can also be the result of a single regal mind, or a small group of minds, and such autocratic governments tend to be tyrannical, but those laws nevertheless originate outside of your own mind, and the way to determine if they are good guides is to use reason. Instinct and law are past judgments while reason is present judgment. When you are making a moral decision, you have three "minds" at your disposal: instinct, reason, and law. Your rational mind is real; the others are metaphorical.

Your three moral minds are not mechanical producers of goodness. They are guides. You can't use them to "give a little whistle" and presto, Jiminy Cricket jumps out with a little umbrella saying, "Do this!" Any one of those three moral minds—or all three—can be faulty. Many of our biological instincts are nurturing, but some are thoughtlessly violent. Reasoning may be based on untested premises or inadequate information, resulting in bad conclusions. Many laws derive from primitive tribal fears or the privilege of power and may have nothing to do with morality. In order for any instinctive, law-abiding, or rational action to be considered morally good, we have to know what "good" means. Speaking about morality, good is the absence of harm. To be good is to act with the intention of minimizing harm

What else is meant by morality? Morality is not a huge mystery. Ethics is simply concerned with reducing harm. (There is a difference between ethics and morality—one is theory and the other is practice— but most people informally use the two words as synonyms, so I will too. Some nonbelievers don't even think we need the word "morality," and they have a point, but I am using the word in the informal sense of "how should we act?") Morality is not a code. It is not following rules or orders. It is not belief or dogma. It is not pleasing an authority figure. It is not "bringing glory" to a god, religion, tribe, or nation. It is not passing a test of virtue. It is not hoping to be told someday that "you are my good and faithful servant." Humanistic morality is the attempt to avoid or lessen harm.[4] It is the only real morality because it uses human values in the natural world, not "spirit values" in a supernatural world, as its measure. It is the opposite of religious morality because it is based on real harm, not the imaginary concepts of "sin" and "holiness."

People should be judged by their actions, not their beliefs. Actions speak louder than faith.

I think most believers are good people. Although religious doctrine is generally irrational, divisive, and irrelevant to human values, some religions have good teachings sprinkled in with the dogma, and many well-meaning believers, to their credit, concentrate on those teachings. Surveying the smorgasbord of belief systems, we notice that they occasionally talk about peace and love. Who would argue with that? Sermons and holy books may encourage charity, mercy, and compassion, even sometimes fairness. These are wonderful ideas, but they are not unique to any religion. We might judge one religion to be better than another, but notice what we are doing. When we judge a religion, we are applying a standard outside of the religion. We are assuming a framework against which religious teachings and practices can be measured. That standard is the harm principle. If a teaching leans toward harm, we judge it as bad. If it leans away from harm, it is good, or at least better than the others. If a religious precept happens to be praiseworthy it is not because of the religion but in spite of it. Its moral worth is measured against real consequences, not orthodoxy or righteousness.

The so-called Golden Rule, for example, is not a bad teaching. It shows up in many religions. Confucius had a version of it long before Christianity, and phrased better: "Do not impose on others what you do not wish for yourself." The value of this obviously humanistic teaching derives not from being found within a religious tradition, but from its emphasis on actions, not faith or dogma. Confucius's wording is better than the Christian "do unto others" because it stresses the *avoidance* of actions that cause harm, which is what Mere Morality is all about. ("Do unto others" is decidedly *not* a good rule for masochists, psychopaths, or people with kinky sexual preferences, religious obsessions, or simply bad taste.) Religious groups such as Buddhists, Jains, and Quakers that are known for their ideals (if not always practices) of pacifism are more moral than groups such as Christian Crusaders, Muslim suicide bombers, and Kamikaze pilots, whose dogma has led directly to violence. We can make this judgment on the basis of lessening harm, which is a principle available to all of us.

So the good values that a religion might profess are not religious values. They are human values. They transcend religion, not in a supernatural sense, but in the natural sense that they are available to everyone, regardless of our particular religious heritages or choices. They are shared across humanity, and what makes them good is their humanism, not their theology. This means that the purely religious values—the ones that make a religion unique and supposedly "better" than the others—are not good values, because they are irrelevant to morality. What day of the week you should worship, how many times you should say a certain prayer, what religious texts you should memorize, how you should dress, whether women should wear jewelry or makeup in church (or whether their bodies should be seen at all), what words you can say or pictures you can draw or songs you can sing, what books you should read or music you should listen to or movies you should watch, what foods you should eat, whether you can drink alcohol or caffeine, whether women can take positions of leadership, if and how women should submit to men, how women should control their own reproductive future, who your children are allowed to date or marry, how gays, nonconformists, heretics, or infidels should be dealt with, how a class of privileged leaders (clergy) should be treated or addressed or whether they should be allowed to marry, how much of your money or time is demanded by the religion, how many times a day you should pray, what words should be said or what direction you should face during prayer, what incantations should be performed during certain rites like baptism and death, what side of the bed you should get out of, what specific doctrines you should believe, what "holy books" or scriptures are true, whether a snake actually spoke human language or a man was born of a virgin, how science should be viewed, whether the earth is six thousand or four billion years old, what was the true nature of the founder of your religion, and so on—all of those beliefs that differ among religions are morally irrelevant, or worse.

Purely religious teachings are most often divisive and dangerous. They build walls between people, creating artificial social conflicts, prejudice, and discrimination. They have started wars and fueled persecutions. One bloody example was the violent Thirty Years' War in Europe, which had many causes but primarily began as a conflict between Lutherans and Catholics over infant baptism, transubstantiation, and whether prayers to the Heavenly Father need an intermediary.

If religious teachings cause unnecessary harm—and they often do— they are immoral and should be denounced. If we play C. S. Lewis's game and separate out common human morality, Mere Morality, from religion, nothing is left worth praising on ethical grounds. (We might appreciate religious art or music, for example, but this is irrelevant to morality.) Turn it around and strip each religion of its weird supernatural and ritualistic uniqueness and what is left, if anything—such as peace, love, joy, charity, and reciprocal altruism—is Mere Morality, or humanistic goodness.

We don't need religion to be good. Religion actually gets in the way. Getting rid of purely religious mandates makes life simpler and safer. Rejecting religion filters out the noise to bring a clarity of judgment, making it easier to be a good atheist than a good Christian.

Since harm is natural, not supernatural, its avoidance is a material exercise. Harm is a threat to survival. It is disease, predators, parasites, toxins, invasion, war, violence, theft, parental neglect, pollution of the environment, excessive heat, cold, lack of food, water, shelter, and adequate clothing, unsafe working conditions, accidents, drowning, natural disasters such as floods, earthquakes, volcanos, winds, storms, lightning, mudslides, coastal erosion . . . you can add to this list, but whatever you add will be natural. If your intention is to end up with less harm—real natural harm, not imaginary "sin," which is supposedly offending the so-called holiness of an egotistical fictional father figure—then you are acting morally. And this is true even if you fail; if you truly intend to lessen harm—and the law, for example, considers intention as much as the actual act—then you will learn from your mistakes.

Intention is crucial when determining the legality or morality of an action. If you trespass on my property and trample through my garden while fleeing from an attacker, I will not press charges. If you do it because you hate my family, then I will press charges. In the first case, I can see that my garden is minimal collateral damage in the overall assessment of harm. In the second case, it is maximal harm, in context.

In assessing harm, it is the overall consequences that matter, not just personal desires. People who are selfish, greedy, and egotistical may indeed be trying to minimize the harm to their own personal lives, but if they are ignoring the harm their actions cause to others, they are not acting morally. That is what morality means. That is why we have laws against theft, homicide, battery, abuse, mayhem, and perjury. Mere Morality does not mean we should completely ignore our own interests; it means we should take *all* harm into account. If an action results in a harm that is much greater to yourself than to another person or persons, then it is not immoral for you to protect yourself. That's why we allow for the motive of self-defense in a trial.

On the other hand, although it might be unwise and unhealthy for you to choose to harm *yourself*, the question of whether it is moral only arises if it affects other people. If you burn a $100 bill that you own, that might be stupid, but it is not theft. If you burn *my* $100 bill, it is immoral. Morality is social. Harm is still harm, whether it is social or not, but your body is your body, and if you are mentally healthy, and if your action does not affect others, and if you can cover your own health expenses, then harming yourself is a health issue for you alone, not a moral issue for society. It should be none of my business what you do to yourself. (Although, if you are my friend, I may try to talk you out of it.) If a man cuts off one of his own fingers (or some other body part, as Jesus encouraged in Matthew 19:11–12[5]), that is certainly harmful and destructive, and may be unhealthy, but the act is only *immoral* if it affects other people—and it might indeed, especially if others are dependent on that person. (In my case, as a professional pianist, it would certainly affect others.) If I know in advance that that man is intending to lose a finger, and I suspect there is no good reason for it, then I am the one faced with the moral question of whether I should try to stop him. I certainly want to keep people from harming themselves, and I think most of us feel that way. But if the person is not mentally unhealthy, then what he is doing might actually be a moral act, as in the case of the Russian men who shot off their trigger fingers in order to avoid being drafted to fight in a war not of their choosing, preferring to stay home and raise their families. Similarly, virtually all women who choose to have an abortion are making a mentally healthy and rational choice, a difficult decision for moral and health reasons. I'm not directly comparing a fetus to a finger, although most abortions occur when the fetus is smaller than the tip of your little finger. Contrary to the dogmatic opinions of the misnamed "pro-lifers," abortion is not killing an unborn baby. (See chapter 3 for more on abortion.) The blinkered absolutist doctrine of some religious groups that "life begins at conception" interferes with moral reasoning, and in this case, those believing buttinskis should butt out. They should learn what real morality means.

And, by the way, when Jesus announced that we should cut off body parts, he was telling others to harm themselves. There were entire monastic orders that castrated themselves because Jesus said in Matthew 19:12 that "he that is able to receive it, let him receive it." Every year in the United States we read about one or two men who mutilate themselves in order to prove their obedience to Christ. In my opinion, *that* is immoral.

Mental illness or instability are not "evil" or immoral. The consequences of the actions of mentally deficient people may indeed be harmful, but we put such people in the hospital, not in prison. It is a health issue, not a moral issue. For society, however, mental illness is indeed a moral issue because those who are entrusted with the authority to determine the fate of such individuals have to determine the course of action that results in the least amount of overall harm to society as well as to the individual involved.

So it all comes down to harm. Mere Morality uses the three minds of instinct, reason, and law to judge harm. Improving on the New Testament, we might say, "Now abideth instinct, law, and reason, but the greatest of these is reason." For most toddlers, instinct is central; for most believers, law is central; but a mature and free human being knows that if reason is not the final arbiter, instinct and law are useless, even dangerous. The three minds have to cooperate. Remember, I'm not suggesting you have three little minds within your own brain, only that instinct and law are the results of minds other than your own. Instinct and law prejudge your actions, but reason, the real-time investigator, can re-judge them, using the harm principle as the measure.

All three of these tools, taken together, can make a powerful arsenal for moral decisions. For better or worse, they are all we have.

The first moral mind, on the left shoulder, is instinct. When I caught that falling baby it was a physical, biological impulse. There was no time for conscious reasoning, but there must have been some quick subconscious calculation. Obviously, my brain had to grasp the situation, "concluding" that a harm was about to occur, anticipating what would have happened if nobody intervened. I put "concluding" in quotes because it seems weird to think of the subconscious mind deliberating to reach a logical conclusion, though something like that must have happened. I must have instantly surveyed the space around me and known it was clear enough and close enough for me to act. But I don't remember any of that. Everything unfolded before I thought about it, below the level of consciousness. Some might call the subconscious decision to act "premoral" or "prerational," but whatever you call it, it worked. The point is that it had to be quick. "An immediate reflexive action," writes Robert Burton, "has clear evolutionary benefits over more time-consuming conscious perception and deliberation."[6] Speed of action gave an edge to those ancestors of ours who became successful enough to breed and raise successful offspring. It is one of the reasons you are here. It is a direct inheritance from your long-forgotten multi-great-grandparents, and if you have children it is part of what you will bequeath to them. Those instincts increase the odds of survival.

On its face that sounds cold and impersonal, as if evolution were simply a massive calculating machine, but inside my mind, inside my body, it *feels* like caring. I experienced compassion when I grabbed that baby carrier. And the fact that it feels good is part of the mechanism for propagating life. We now know that acts of charity and compassion actually boost pleasure chemicals in the brain, similar to how we feel when eating chocolate, listening to music, making love, or laughing. Why do you hold the door open for the person coming behind you? It's partly learned common courtesy, but it's more than that. You don't know that person, and might not even like that person. It's not just reciprocal altruism—"Listen, buddy, you better hold the door for *me* next time!"—because you would do it anyway. You would feel bad not doing it. Why? Part of it is pure instinct, part of it is chosen social cooperation, and part of it is the little chemical kick in the head when you help others. We crave doing good, most of us. "These good acts give us pleasure," wrote Thomas Jefferson, "but how happens it that they give us pleasure? Because nature hath implanted in our breasts a love of others, a sense of duty to them, a moral instinct, in short, which prompts us irresistibly to feel and to succor their distresses."[7]

Thomas Jefferson was a deist, living just like an atheist with no religious practices, but believing there had to be some kind of starter god, or impersonal force that got everything going. The deists were the pre-Darwinian freethinkers, lacking a model for the origin of life. But Jefferson got it right about instincts, anticipating the theory of evolution by many decades. Charles Darwin famously wrote: "It has, I think, now been shewn that man and the higher animals, especially the Primates, have some few instincts in common. All have the same senses, intuitions, and sensations,—similar passions, affections, and emotions, even the more complex ones, such as jealousy, suspicion, emulation, gratitude, and magnanimity; they practise deceit and are revengeful; they are sometimes susceptible to ridicule, and even have a sense of humour; they feel wonder and curiosity; they possess the same faculties of imitation, attention, deliberation, choice, memory, imagination, the association of ideas, and reason, though in very different degrees. The individuals of the same species graduate in intellect from absolute imbecility to high excellence. They are also liable to insanity, though far less often than in the case of man."[8] Scientists today continue to prove that Darwin and Jefferson were right. We are discovering that the same "moral instincts" are found in other animals, though to different degrees, as Darwin noticed. All species have evolved instincts that enhance the survival of their genes—they wouldn't be here otherwise—and this often involves behavior that is cooperative, altruistic, and sacrificial. Frans de Waal, in his book *The Age of Empathy: Nature's Lessons for a Kinder Society*, gives many examples of nonhuman animals acting compassionately. Altruism is an evolved behavior that does not rely solely on having a "higher" brain that can construct formal moral philosophies. Chimpanzees will sacrifice for each other. They will lag behind to help a wounded companion, licking their wounds, putting their own lives in danger to protect a weaker individual. They work together cooperatively. They hug and express emotions of love, gratitude, sorrow, and empathy. Chimpanzees are primates like us, but altruism also occurs within species less closely related to humans.

De Waal tells a story in which an underwater mine exploded prematurely, temporarily stunning a dolphin, who began sinking to the bottom. Two other dolphins came to its rescue, swimming on each side of their distressed companion, placing their bodies under its fins and lifting it to the surface where it could breathe long enough to recover. Whales and elephants are also highly intelligent and show empathy for each other. When wolves get too rough in their play with each other, they will back off and crouch and "apologize" to the injured party. Such acts even occur across species. A dog was seen swimming out to rescue a drowning seal. Dolphins were observed ushering a drowning dog to safety. A chimpanzee was seen trying to help a bird with a broken wing fly. There are many examples of animals from one species protecting and nurturing the young of other species.

Dogs appear to express moral emotions like shame, or an eagerness to help (such as compassion).[9] Many of us consider our pets to be members of the family, sensitive to each other's desires, needs, and moods. If you have an animal in your household, don't you consider it to be more than just a "pet"? (You will read about our amazing pet cockatiel in the last chapter.) We can't pretend that they are exactly like humans, but neither should we conclude they are completely alien or inferior. All species on earth share common genes, and since those surviving genes are the result of ancestors in similar environments needing to protect themselves from harm, it makes sense that there would be a biological continuum, a family tree with common traits. We humans are part of that tree.

You might object that the appearance of animal morality is just a thoughtless expression of an automatic instinct and that we could also give numerous examples of animals *not* caring about each other. But we could say the same thing about humans. The fact is that some of our moral behavior is rooted in our genes. (Of course, everything is ultimately genetic, but some features are more hard-coded while others are more flexible, open to modification by nurture and the environment.) I think empathy, however it is described and whatever cluster of genes or brain circuits it involves, is one of those characteristics of a species that vary across the population, just like any other trait that shows up in a rough bell curve distribution. We humans also show cross-species compassion, but it varies. Some people break into tears when they see cruelty to animals, and if you are like my sister-in-law Suzan, you will break into a rage. But others, on the other side of the bell curve, are not distressed to see such suffering. There are also a few people at the tail end of the curve who actually enjoy seeing animals suffer.[10] Most of us fall somewhere in the middle. This may be true in other species as well, with their curves shifted one way or another relative to other species. So yes, we likely recognize less moral sentiment or moral reasoning among other animals—or at least behavior that appears moral, because we can't use language to ask them if their subjective inner feelings are emotional or cognitive, or a mix like ours—but we do see some. The fact that some human animals are uncaring sociopaths and psychopaths does not make us an amoral species.

Many religious believers are taught that other animals don't have "souls" (whatever that means) so they cannot be considered moral in the same way humans are, but that is proving the point. Whatever happens in the brains of other species, moral *behavior* does exist, to some degree, regardless of how conscious the individual might be. Some argue that other animals are indeed conscious, perhaps to a lesser degree, but that is beside the point. Instinct is biological, whether there is a "soul" or not.[11] The evidence of empathy and altruism in other species shows that we are connected to a web of life from which our behavioral instincts arise. Many animals have impulses or desires to lessen harm, and humans are no exception. Most of us will instinctively catch a falling baby and hold the door open for the person behind us without much thought.

This does not mean we are slaves to our instincts. "There is no reason," writes Jerry Coyne, "to see ourselves as marionettes dancing on the strings of evolution. Yes, certain parts of our behavior may be genetically encoded, instilled by natural selection in our savanna-dwelling ancestors. But genes aren't destiny."[12] Most of the time we can check our instincts.

Treating instinct as a "moral mind," or part of the psyche, looks somewhat like the Id in Freud's model. Freud admitted there is no such "thing" as "the Id," as I admit that instinct is not really a "moral mind." The Id and the moral mind are both ways to metaphorically visualize the set of hard-wired and soft-wired biological instincts that we are all born with. We have many instincts—some nurturing, some violent—and they often conflict with each other. But Freud did not think the Id was moral in itself. He thought it was something for the Ego and Superego to control. Freud's view was closer to having a devil on your shoulder, while my view is more like having a well-meaning friend on your shoulder—someone you want to consult but not always agree with. I simply want to emphasize that instincts are more than just disorganized uncontrollable impulses. Since the instincts of our social species evolved for a reason, they can be respected as a part of the moral process.

Daniel Dennett, in *Freedom Evolves,* writes that it makes no difference whether our moral impulses are evolved or learned. "[T]he theory that explains morality . . . should be neutral with regard to whether our moral attitudes, habits, preferences, and proclivities are a product of genes or culture." I think this is true because culture itself is ultimately a product of evolution. Whether you think "instinct" is purely biological or a learned habit, or a combination of the two, it comes down to the same goal: the minimization of harm to biological organisms.

The second moral mind, between your shoulders, is reason. It is the mind you care most about—what makes you feel you are a free volitional agent—since reason is a function of your own brain, not the brains of your ancestors or the collective mind of society. It is the part that makes deliberate conscious decisions. Along with your animal instincts, reason helps determine whether or not your genes will pass on to future descendants, not to mention whether you will have a chance at a good life yourself.

In addition to the "lower" dispositions that we share with other animals—and I put that word in quotes because "lower" does not mean "lesser," but "earlier evolved"—we also possess a large neocortex with a recently developed frontal lobe that give us a much greater ability to deliberate before making decisions. (By the way, I think this is a big part of what is meant by consciousness and "free will": the attempt to anticipate the future.) "Humans usually have considered themselves to be different and apart from the other animals," writes Bernd Heinrich in *The Mind of the Raven.* "Perhaps, as lion researcher Craig Packer points out in his book *Into Africa,* that is because 'we make it all up as we go along,' whereas an ant has 'every small instruction laid out in advance.'"[13] Since none of the other animals have such a proportionately large and complicated brain, they are, as far as we know, unable to construct a formal moral philosophy, but this does not mean they lack altruism, empathy, or moral sentiments. It means they are less flexible than humans, relying more on instinct than analysis. Other animals generally have access to fewer or simpler tools than we humans use in making moral decisions. Your neocortex ("neo" means "new") is a "higher" brain that gives you the ability to reason. (And "higher," of course, does not mean "better," but "with a more recently evolved layer of complexity.")

A useful if overly simple way to say this is that the lower brain gives you instincts while the higher brain gives you reason. That is simplistic because the levels are certainly not starkly demarcated or isolated. They obviously work as a whole much of the time, but it is clear that there is a difference, if only in the fact that the conscious mind is the only part you are immediately fully aware of. If you have time to deliberate, you can use reason to help judge how to act. In fact, you *must* use reason, otherwise you are not a fully aware moral agent.

Reason is not a thing. It is a function of the brain. Our brains have a hugely complex new layer, or set of layers, that have evolved to the point where we now have the ability to use language and to think more broadly about our behavior. We can think about our thoughts. We can think about thinking about our thoughts. We can think about other people thinking about us thinking about their thoughts. (This is sometimes called Theory of Mind.) We can deliberate, compare, anticipate, contrast, imagine, and prioritize. We can run "what if" scenarios. We can refrain from acting and wait for more information. (That is one of the functions of the frontal lobe, which checks our actions in social settings. It is what keeps you from burping loudly at a wedding or funeral, for example.) We can investigate, read, and ask for help. We can search our memories for consequences to similar situations, past lessons, previous mistakes.

But all of this takes time. If we don't have the time, we fall back on instinct, or on law (see below), but if we do have time, we can contemplate. An impulse is not always the best course of action. Malcolm Gladwell, in his book *Blink: The Power of Thinking Without Thinking*, and Gerd Gerzinger, in *Gut Feelings: The Intelligence of the Unconscious*, show that very often we simply "know" what to do intuitively, without deliberation. A hunch can be a signal from your lower biological brain to your higher consciousness that something is wrong, though you can't put it into words. Your "gut feeling" happens somewhere beneath your conscious awareness, but it is no less important than reason. Instincts are a huge advantage, but Gladwell and Gerzinger also give examples of gut feelings gone wrong. Animal instincts are valuable not because they are *always* right but because they were advantageous most of the time when they were being naturally selected. "I'm not a textbook player. I'm a gut player," President George W. Bush told Bob Woodward about his disastrous decision to go to war in Iraq. Gut feelings can go horribly wrong sometimes—especially when they are prompted by religion rather than evidence—because they are firing in a different environment from which they originally evolved. But we have those instinctive feelings for a reason. Your gut feelings evolved to point usually in the right direction, away from threats, but evolutionary adaptations only need to be more successful on average, not in every single instance. If you want to improve the odds, and if you have time, then you will naturally want to use the newly evolved tool of reason to evaluate your gut feelings to help pick the most morally justified action. Your reason might conclude that your impulse or the law in any particular case might not be the best governor of your behavior. It might tell you that your previous decisions or habits are inappropriate in a new situation. A heroic instinct might be admirable, but it might also be fatal.

What if the falling baby had just been a doll? What if the floor were wet? What if I had lunged for the baby carrier only to break some of her bones, or mine? Or worse? In those cases, my intention would have been honorable but my action might have been counterproductive. I might have injured a bystander. Our instincts can benefit from a careful appraisal of the situation, if there is time. A lifeguard once told me that unless you are a trained lifesaver, or an excellent swimmer with a lot of experience, you should resist the urge to jump in to save a drowning person in a hazardous situation. (If you are like me, you might have a hard time holding back.) Sometimes such actions result in two tragedies instead of one. Call for help. Don't become a dead hero. Yet the fact that most of us have these automatic impulses to do good tells us something about our human nature.

So assuming you have the time to think things through (and you often do), how does your reason determine what is moral? Mere Morality boils down to a simple process: compare the relative merits of the consequences of your available actions and try to pick the course that results in the least amount of harm. That's all there is to it. Try to lessen harm. Of course, there is more to a full ethical life than that—generosity, charity, increasing beauty and knowledge, enhancing health and life style, improving the environment and living conditions, and so on—but when it comes to basic moral dilemmas, use reason to identify the harm and you will know how to proceed.

Morality is not a code. It is a compass. A compass does not tell you where you are or where to go; it only shows you where north is. Think of north as the direction of less harm and south as more harm. If your actions are heading more to the north, then you are acting morally. Of course, you can't always travel directly north—the terrain is often complicated and actions can conflict with each other, and you might have to detour east, west, or even south for a while—but if you intend your general path to go more northerly than southerly, your journey is moral. (No offense to my friends in Australia, Brazil, and South Africa! If you live below the equator, then head south.)

I said above that morality is a simple process, and that is true. It is easy in principle, but usually not in practice. Life is messy. The compass is simple, but the course can be winding. You often don't fully know what consequences to realistically expect, or how to weight them for comparison. The lesser of two roughly equal evils or the greater of two roughly equal goods can be hard to judge. As I asked in my children's book *Maybe Right, Maybe Wrong,* should I vote for Stinky or Bully? And it gets tougher when there are more than two variables, or when you don't know all the options or consequences, or you don't have experience with such a situation, or when you are not as informed as you could be. But if you are truly desiring to minimize overall harm, then you will want to learn, to educate yourself as much as possible about what happens in the real world. Look before you leap.

Mere Morality might look like utilitarianism—"the greatest happiness of the greatest number," as philosopher Jeremy Bentham put it—but it is not, because it is at the level of individual social interaction, not society as a whole, nor is it concerned primarily with happiness. Utilitarianism goes beyond Mere Morality. Of course, happiness is what we all want, if we are mentally healthy, but I don't think it is my moral responsibility to make you or anyone else happy. My minimal responsibility (if I want to act morally) is to simply try to remove as many unnecessary obstructions as I can from our freedom to seek happiness. (Maybe the mere freedom to seek happiness is a happiness in itself? The old joke asks: "If the purpose of life is to make others happy, what is *their* purpose in life?") Bentham, by the way, was a firm nonbeliever and a proponent of state-church separation. "No power of government," he wrote, "ought to be employed in the endeavor to establish any system or article of belief on the subject of religion. . . . [I]n no instance has a system in regard to religion been ever established, but for the purpose, as well as with the effect of its being made an instrument of intimidation, corruption, and delusion, for the support of depredation and oppression in the hands of governments."[14] Neither is Mere Morality a negative utilitarianism: the least harm for the greatest number. I don't know if I am capable or qualified enough to calculate the greatest good, or least harm, for the greatest number. How do we assign weightings in such a grand calculation? That sounds like a job for a government (see below), and even governments, with all their resources, have trouble figuring it out.

Mere Morality is definitely consequentialist, although I think it is not just the ends that justify the means. The means also need to be justified by reason: they must involve the minimal amount of harm necessary for the task. That means that the ends *are* the means: the goal of minimizing harm should be accomplished with minimal harm. You might have to amputate a limb to save a life. You might stick a needle into a screaming baby in order to give it a life-saving injection. You might need to neutralize an attacker with harmful defensive weapons. If you are trying to get the job done with the least amount of damage, you are acting morally. That's what morality means.

In his book *The Moral Landscape*, Sam Harris identifies the "well-being" of conscious creatures as the aim of morality. I think that is right. "Well-being" is perhaps a more positive way to characterize the harm principle, but it boils down to the same thing. All through Sam's thoughtful book, when "well-being" is unpacked with real-life examples, they always involve the avoidance of some kind of harm or limitation. Well, you can't be "well" if you are harmed.

Mere Morality judges actions by their overall results, so I think we should simply call it the "harm principle," and only call it "utilitarian" when applied at a global level. I do recycle my trash, but my action is so insignificant in the big picture that it only makes sense if huge numbers of people do it, which is part of the third moral mind: law and society.

The third moral mind, on the right shoulder, is not located in dead ancestors or individual consciousness, but in the social agreements formed by the large tribe to which we belong. Remember that I am not suggesting that law is actually one of your own minds: in a democratic society, humanistic law is a result of a collective mind (including yours) that expresses itself as social expectation or obligation. Unless you live alone on one of the moons of Saturn, the laws you encounter come from somewhere other than your own conscious mind.

In the "revealed" religions such as Judaism, Christianity, and Islam, humanity is judged by the law. In a humanistic society, the law is judged by humanity. Many holier-than-thou believers strongly feel they are minimizing harm when they fight reforms like abortion and gay rights. Their church feeds them the dogma that certain things are abominations, not based on any real harm to humans, but on supposedly divinely revealed commandments that declare them to be offensive to the "holiness" of the creator. Their "morality" is otherworldly. Since their principles are not based on real harm, their actions often cause more damage than good. Religious authoritarians are pests that invade our households with superstition and fear. They replace reason with faith. Reason shows us, for example, that there is nothing wrong with being gay, and if the bible says homosexuality is wrong, then the bible is wrong, not homosexuality. These people are free to have faith and live by their own rules. They are even welcome to try to persuade the rest of us to think like them, but in a secular society, they are not free to impose their theocratic beliefs on everyone else by law.

The law does not originate outside of humanity. The making of prescriptive laws is a human action and is therefore subject to the same scrutiny as any other action.[15] Mere Morality does not require that we blindly follow or respect the law, only that we acknowledge it. Not all laws in the world are democratically decided, and not all laws are good. Many are completely unnecessary, and others are harmful. Moral decisions require freedom of choice, and authoritarianism is the opposite of such freedom. Not all societies progress. Some laws, even in a democratic society, are the result of special interest groups gaining political power and forcing legislators to protect or promote their own narrow agenda. This is especially true with laws pertaining to religion.

Whatever country you live in, any law based on "glory" instead of real harm is dangerous. The glory of the nation, or the glory of the monarchy, or the glory of the superior race, or the glory of the church have been the cause of horrible wars and legally sanctioned discrimination. Any laws based solely on these glories should be morally denounced. They cause unnecessary harm.

Mere Morality simply acknowledges the law as a kind of prejudged head start. After looking at the law, reason can judge whether its prescriptions are good or bad in a particular situation. Moral decisions are sounder when they are better informed, so we need to know what the law says. If you are fortunate enough to live in a secular society, one that is progressing via humanistic principles (not sovereign commandments), then the law can be a useful educational guide. The law ideally represents a group wisdom that has already been thought through in advance, based on experiences and data that you might not possess personally. You don't always have to reinvent the wheel.

Most of us rarely bump into the law. If we are reasonable, fair, and kind, we don't need it. The real value of law is for those people who sometimes do not (or cannot) use reason. Criminal law, for example, is largely concerned with correcting those thoughtless instinctive impulses we inherited from our often violent ancestors. Picture the three moral minds: instinct on one shoulder, law on the other, and reason in the middle. If reason doesn't temper your impulses, then law will hop over and try to do it. In other words, if you can't handle yourself, society (for its own protection) will do it for you. But remember that reason sits in the middle: reason can judge *both* instinct and law.

I think I know how to handle an automobile—don't we all? But when I am on a public road, I watch for the speed limit. I realize that the speed limit is not a hard-and-fast limitation of physics, like the speed of light. In most circumstances, I could usually drive safely much faster than the posted speed. But I also know there are good reasons for the state to impose a law on how fast I drive on a road that is owned and used by all of us. I may not know all those reasons. They probably have to do with efficient traffic flow, public safety, and convenience. In the absence of a true emergency (such as rushing a heart attack victim to the hospital), I willingly surrender part of my moral decision-making to the collective mind of society.

When we say that "the state" is imposing a law, we are not personifying the state as a single person, at least not in the United States. The state is all of us, our collective judgment. A democratic government is not a dictatorship, not a single mind handing down decrees. A "collective mind" is not a single group consciousness: it is the result of the pooling and sifting of the judgment of many minds.

"The state" is an idealized concept. In reality lawmaking is often a sloppy power struggle between special interests resulting in compromises, pork barreling, policies based on ideology rather than human needs, and bad experiments that need fixing. I think for many people "the state" is a "thing," attaining a life of its own, becoming a surrogate for monarchy or religion, not truly representing all of us who have entrusted our leadership with the responsibility to govern wisely. But this valid libertarian critique of government does not undermine Mere Morality; it strengthens it. It gives reason a job to do.

Any law can be changed if enough of us agree. We could make the speed limit 100 miles per hour if we wanted to. However, since minimizing harm is a primary goal of traffic laws, the speed limit ought to be informed by science, which should consider such factors as the physics of surface coefficients, the safety features of vehicles and roadways, and the driving habits of the average person—factors which deal with real harm in the real world.[16] The only laws that can't be changed—or shouldn't be changed—in the United States are those based on liberties or restrictions specifically hardwired into the Constitution, such as the freedom of speech, religion, press, assembly, and petition and the limitations on government to abridge those freedoms. Those values are so basic to our lives that it seems unlikely that a supermajority of us would choose to get rid of them by amending the Constitution.

Our collective moral mind has agreed on laws and principles that are good for most of us most of the time. Obeying those laws more often results in less harm. You might be a very good driver, much better than the average, but you can't deny the fact that if something unexpected happened while you were driving 100 miles per hour on a road shared by all of us—if a deer or child ran out in front of you, or a truck swerved due to a blowout, or you hit a patch of invisible ice—the resulting accident would be more deadly at that speed than at 50 miles per hour. Your individual freedom has to be tempered for the common good. If you don't like that, stay off the highway.

Of course, democracy is no guarantee of morality. If a majority of people in a state lacking constitutional rights and liberties are theocratic, for example, they could vote to limit freedoms—they could use democracy to destroy democracy—not with the intention of minimizing real harm but to protect themselves from the manufactured harm of having their religious opinions challenged. That is why I think the best hope, the only hope, for a peaceful world is secular government.

Breaking the law is not in itself immoral. Humanistic morality judges actions by harm, not rules. Sometimes, as in the case of rushing a heart attack victim to the hospital, it would be immoral *not* to break the law, as long you are driving as safely as you can. If you get cited for it, well, pay the ticket; it was worth it. But in general, a secular democratic society—a collective humanistic mind—functions better when the harm principle for a particular action can be applied in advance and announced as an expected behavior that on average will result in less harm for everyone. If everybody else obeys the traffic laws, then *you* are safer. If you don't obey the law, then everybody else is at a higher risk, and "everybody else" (government) is morally justified in trying to modify your behavior through penalties such as a speeding ticket, revoked privileges, or jail time.

It often seems silly, but I almost always wait for the walk sign before crossing the street even when there is no traffic in sight. I am not moralistic about it: if I am with someone else who wants to cross, I will go with them. But I do think obeying the law is moral (assuming it is a good law) in the long run. According to Wisconsin statutes, it is illegal for a pedestrian to go against a "Don't Walk" sign or red light even when there are no vehicles within sight, but it seems most pedestrians and bicyclists where I live feel they are above this law. If someone asks me why I stand there waiting, I reply: "If you were in a car, would you run the red light?" They usually say no, but that is because automobiles are more dangerous, and anyway, nobody enforces jaywalking laws in this town. (Try it in California.)[17] But I have sometimes seen pedestrians seriously misjudge traffic and interfere with automobiles. I estimate that less than one person in twenty stands waiting with me for the light to change, and I suppose the nineteen jaywalkers might have legitimate emergencies—who am I to judge?—but I bet they are not all atheists.

How do we know if a law is a good law? There are many repressive and harmful laws in the world, especially in countries that do not honor humanistic democracy. Blasphemy used to be illegal in many parts of the United States. So too was interracial marriage. What about laws related to homosexuality? Or doctor-assisted suicide? What about stem-cell research, abortion rights, birth control, prostitution, polygamy, military draft, tax laws, nude beaches, animal leash laws, motorcycle helmet laws? What about laws based on religious principles? What sense does it make, for example, to outlaw same-sex marriage or a woman showing her face in public? Those religious laws are simply an attempt to legitimize primitive homophobia, sexism, and sectarian orthodoxy. A truly moral law would deal with such discrimination by aiming at the attackers, not the targets. When considering any law, I think we should simply ask, "What is the harm?" Bad laws increase harm. If following a law more often results in less harm, we can say it is a good law.

We might disagree about what constitutes a good law or when it might be morally justifiable to break the law, but unless you are a complete anarchist (and I am not dissing anarchism, which might work in small groups), you know that individuals in a large group can benefit from the expectation that all or most members of the group will agree, through voluntary assent or persuasive measures, to cooperate with each other to lessen the risk of harm to each and all of us. It is out of respect, maybe even love for my species, that I stand there patiently waiting for the light to change. It's for my own safety as well because I sometimes make mistakes of judgment. Of course, I am not an automaton. I would be willing, even happy, to jaywalk. If there is an emergency, I will switch from the collective moral mind to my own rational mind, or even to instinct: a greater immediate danger can override any one of our moral minds.

A few years ago, I drove three hours to a debate on morality. As usual, I planned the trip with plenty of time to drive the speed limit (and if I am not able to drive the speed limit, am I really in control?), as well as to enjoy the drive and scenery without being rushed. I was listening to language tapes, so it was not time wasted. I couldn't help noticing that some of the cars that sped past me in the fast lane sported the Christian fish symbol or "Pro-Life" bumperstickers. Perhaps they all had a legitimate emergency, but whatever their reasons, they all felt justified in taking the law into their own hands. During the debate that night I mentioned those speeding vehicles and complimented Christians for grasping situational ethics. (That prompted some nervous chuckles from believers and outright laughter from freethinkers.) For all their talk about moral absolutes, most believers know that real-life morality is situational, conditional. Or maybe since there is no Mosaic law that commands, "Thou shalt not speed," traffic laws are negotiable? (Tell that to the highway patrol, or the judge.) Perhaps all of those Christians who sped past me are excellent drivers, but whatever their reason for speeding, their action increased the risk of harm.

If they are caught, they should be happy to be ticketed, since they proclaim such a high respect for the law.

Instinct, reason, and law—the three moral minds—are our guides for minimizing harm and living a good life, but reason is the final arbiter. It is true that human nature possesses instincts that are dangerous as well as helpful, and law can moderate those impulses, but without reason morality boils down to a robotic function. Without reason we are slaves serving a master, computers executing a program, soldiers following orders, believers obeying commandments. A healthy functioning society, where citizens enjoy the right to the "pursuit of happiness," is one that bases its laws on principles, not authority. It is a society whose motto should be "In Reason We Trust."

In April 2010, I debated Mat Staver, dean of Liberty University School of Law in Lynchburg, Virginia, on the topic, "Is American law based on the Ten Commandments?" Staver has intervened for the other side in a couple of lawsuits brought by the Freedom From Religion Foundation, so we were truly adversaries, philosophically and legally. The cordial debate took place in their law school's Supreme Courtroom, designed to be a replica of the United States Supreme Court. During the debate, I joked that I coveted that room, but then realized that would be a crime. Trying to connect the dots between American law and the Ten Commandments, Staver mentioned the theocratic laws of the early colonists, Sunday "blue laws," the importance of the bible in swearing an oath in court (perjury laws coming straight from scripture, he claimed), and so on. Straying from the stated topic, he argued that American law is merely "influenced by," not based on, the Ten Commandments. (So I won the debate by default.)

I pointed out that only three of the Ten Commandments—killing, perjury, and theft—have any relevance to modern American law. "If you get 30 percent on your final exam," I asked the students, "what kind of a grade is that?" My opening statement included these words:

> I am going to break the law, and I want all of you to witness. The god of the bible, if he exists, is an evil, immoral, selfish, arrogant, jealous, brutal, bloodthirsty bully, and if he created hell, he can go to hell. I am not saying "God Damn It," I am saying "Damn God." There. I just broke the Third Commandment. I took the name of the Lord Your God in vain. Are you going to have me arrested for blasphemy?[18]

Mat, after complaining that my statement was insulting and shocking, agreed that I should not be arrested for blasphemy in a country that protects free speech. He admitted that there is no law or maxim that America should be based on the Ten Commandments, that he would not favor enacting such laws, and that America should not become a theocracy. He was making my case: American law is *not* based on the bible.[19]

Law does not need or have "a basis." It has ancestors. There is no ultimate or transcendent object out there upon which the law rests. Law—good law, humanistic law—is continuously evolving from earlier experiments as a society improves. Societies don't always improve, of course, but when they do, the adoption of just and fair laws is one of the ways we know it. There used to be a time in our nation when racism, sexism, and classism were perfectly natural and legal—slavery, denying the vote to women, privileged inequality, for example (which are biblically based)—but through struggle and experiment, we have abandoned those primitive harmful practices. Much of that struggle was against the church. Useful laws are not handed to us from outside the universe, written on divinely inscribed slabs of stone. They are human creations. They stem from rebellion, not revelation. The Roman plebeians revolted against the patricians, protesting the abuses of power, and came to a negotiated understanding of equality under the law, due process, innocence until proven guilty, and so on, long before they had contact with Christianity or the Ten Commandments. The laws that arose from the struggle to increase fairness and reduce harm were humanistic, not religious. When they were codified, they were written down not by edict, but with reason.

For some strange reason, twenty-first-century theocrats in the United States are fond of referring to the Magna Carta as a religious basis or predecessor of our Constitution. It was no such thing. It was an ancestor of modern law, much like the little mammals scurrying for survival during the age of dinosaurs were primitive ancestors of the human race. The Magna Carta was the product of thirteenth-century barons rebelling against the authority and excesses of the king, and although it contained some formalistic introductory religious wording, it made no reference to the Commandments or the bible as its "basis." There is nothing in the bible about habeas corpus or due process, for example. Most of the laws in the Magna Carta are irrelevant to Christianity—such as deciding where bridges should be built, or where you can fish in the Thames, or how much knights should be paid—and although a few sections roughly parallel teachings found in the bible (and it would be surprising if they did not, back in those times), no scripture verse is ever cited as a basis for the law. The Magna Carta does not say anything about rights being granted by a creator. In fact, it is the other way around, actually granting rights to God: "Know that we . . . have granted to God and by this our present Charter have confirmed . . . that the English church shall be free." American law does owe a debt to the Magna Carta, but not for biblical reasons.

Neither did English common law, another ancestor, have reference to the bible or the Ten Commandments. Thomas Jefferson concluded that "Christianity neither is, nor ever was a part of the common law."[20] It was originally a jumble of regional legal decisions based on common sense and precedent that roughly came together after a long evolution of trial and error. It is not based on written statutes but on the "survival of the fittest" ideas that had been naturally selected by experience. The prohibition of murder, for example, is (to this day in England) not based on "Thou shalt not kill" or any other statute, but on the legal decisions of ancestor judges amassed over time into a "common" understanding of how we should best treat each other. That is why it is called "common law."

Many of the original English colonists in America were fleeing government tyranny. Those who were religious called themselves "separatists" and "puritans" because they were rebelling, protesting the abuses of power and the limits to freedom of conscience. They were Protestants, after all, fiercely anti-Catholic enemies of the "whore of Rome," as the pope was routinely labeled. Although the colonies began as mini-theocracies, later generations exercised their own freedom of protest and evolved into a more secular society with broader liberties for all believers and nonbelievers. Look what happened with Harvard, originally a religious school founded by Calvinists to educate preachers ("dreading to leave an illiterate Ministry to the Churches") that grew into a humanistic institution of liberal arts education. The seventeenth-century theocrats, at any rate, did not found the United States of America. It was a century and a half later when our actual founders, not wanting any part of the religious divisiveness of the earlier colonies, continued evolving into a secular democratic republic. The evolution is so advanced today that there is now no longer any question of whether any of those once-despised and disenfranchised Catholics can enjoy full participation in our country, although that was a huge issue when John F. Kennedy, a Catholic, was running for the presidency, prompting him to assure us: "I believe in an America where the separation of church and state is absolute."[21] Today, for better or worse, snubbing the religious laws of the Pilgrims, six of the nine justices on the U.S. Supreme Court are Roman Catholics.

The United States of America was not birthed in prayer, as the religious right repeatedly claims. It was birthed in protest. We kicked the king, dictator, master, sovereign, and Lord out of our affairs, turning government upside down, making "We, the people" the supreme authority. Our Declaration of Independence, which does not govern our country but did present the rationale for rebellion, states emphatically and unbiblically that the power of government is not derived from anything other than "the consent of the governed." American law is not based on any scripture. We produced a completely godless constitution, the first in history to separate religion and government. Written under George Washington, approved by the Senate, and signed by John Adams in 1797, the Treaty of Tripoli says quite clearly: "The Government of the United States is not in any sense founded on the Christian religion." (What part of the phrase "in any sense" don't modern Christian theocrats understand?) U.S. laws do not stem from commandments revealed by a cosmic authority or sovereign monarch. The constitution arose naturally from a group of people struggling to be *free* of authority, not to submit to rules. American citizens are not subjects.[22] We are a proudly rebellious people.

Yet there remain free citizens in this country who want us to forsake evolved progressive reforms and drag us back to the tradition of servitude. They think it is dangerous to acquiesce to secular laws forged in rebellion: they want us to return to the primitive days of submission to the commandments of a dictator. Law does not mean the same thing to biblical Christians that it means to the rest of us. Their law is bible-based, conservative, and stagnant, while humanist law is progressive and free to improve. Theirs is autocratic, based solely on the command of a dictator, while ours is democratic, based on the consent of the governed. Their rules come from otherworldly values, while our principles are based on this world, where morality really matters. Theirs is a put-down of humanity ("original sin"), while ours is a celebration of who we really are ("Bill of Rights"). Their view of human nature is pessimistic, while ours is optimistic and hopeful.

In *Losing Faith in Faith* and *Godless,* I describe the shortcomings of theistic morality, which is based primarily on a might-makes-right mentality. With its threat of eternal torture, inept role models, and a cosmic dictator who is praise-hungry, angry, and violent, the bible offers an ethical system that reduces to the morality of a toddler who fears and flatters the father figure. In most religions, behavior is governed by rules, but in real life behavior should be governed by principles.

Annie Laurie and I were married in 1987 by a judge in a secular wedding at Freethought Hall in Sauk City, Wisconsin. We planned everything to represent our natural freethought views of equality, as well as our love and respect for our families in *this* world, not some imagined supernatural world. My Mom beautifully sang "Embraceable You" in that acoustically pleasing historic building, a song written by the nonbelieving Gershwin brothers. Judge Moria Krueger (who says she owed her judgeship to the fact that Annie Laurie and her mother Anne spearheaded the successful grassroots recall of her predecessor, Judge Archie Simonson, because of his sexist "boys will be boys" defense of a group of high-school gang rapists) performed the egalitarian, feminist ceremony. Annie Laurie kept her birth name, as did I.

So it was a shock to be confronted by the government with religion when we went to the Dane County Courthouse to get our marriage license. The county clerk asked us to raise our right hands for the oath: "Do you solemnly swear that the testimony you shall give in this matter shall be the truth, the whole truth and nothing but the truth, so help you God?" We were caught off guard! We told the clerk that we are atheists, and reminded her that the state allows for a secular affirmation in place of a religious oath.

"Oh," she said, fumbling through her notes. "No one has asked that before." After a half-minute, she said, "Well, do you affirm to tell the truth, so help you God?"

We laughed. "We don't believe in God," we repeated slowly, "so we can't say that!"

She took a moment to look through the statutes, and finally found the alternative wording in 906.03(3): "Do you solemnly, sincerely and truly declare and affirm that the testimony you shall give in this matter shall be the truth, the whole truth and nothing but the truth; and this you do under the pains and penalties of perjury?"

Finally, a secular promise! We said, "Yes."(Proving you can have law without religion). But isn't it interesting that if you don't believe in God you have to be reminded of the punishment of the law? If you do believe in God you can simply say, "so help me, God," and that is enough to warrant honesty. If you don't believe in God, it is assumed you have less motive to tell the truth, the "pains and penalties of perjury" replacing the threat of "hell" to force you to be a good person. We think the statute should be reversed. The secular oath should be preferred (as it is for the presidential oath of office in the U.S. Constitution), and a religious alternative can be available for those who request it. Besides, the clerk should have appreciated our honesty. If an atheist were to swear, "so help me, God," that would be an act of perjury!

Bible believers often twist themselves into pretzels to make their "Good Book" look good. They claim that we degenerate humans need absolute morality bestowed upon us from an ethically superior being, but if you actually read the bible you find little to admire about the devious deity depicted in that document.

As I mention in chapter 1, William Lane Craig is an intelligent and respected Christian debater when it comes to philosophy. His arguments are wrong,[23] but he is not stupid or uninformed. However, when it comes to a discussion of morality, he is truly off the deep end. "In a world without God," Craig writes, "who is to say which values are right and which are wrong? Who is to judge that the values of Adolf Hitler are inferior to those of a saint? The concept of morality loses all meaning in a universe without God. . . . For in a universe without God, good and evil do not exist—there is only the bare valueless fact of existence, and there is no one to say you are right and I am wrong."[24] Well, yes there is, Bill. Hitler was wrong because he caused unnecessary harm. And many saints are wrong for the same reason.

During a radio interview replying to my critiques and Sam Harris's denunciations of the genocidal actions of the biblical deity, Craig came to God's defense:

> God is not bound by the same moral duties that we are. Our moral duties are established by God's commandments to us . . . but God himself doesn't issue commands to himself, so he doesn't stand under the same moral duties that we do. . . . When God commands the Israelites to exterminate the Canaanite clans, they are acting as God's moral agents under his command. So I think that God had the right to command them to do something which, in the absence of a divine command, would have been wrong, but given a divine command it is not wrong. In fact, it becomes their moral duty.[25]

Genocide is a moral duty? How can Craig know that if it would be wrong to do something "in the absence of a divine command," it is only the divine command that makes it right or wrong? Moral actions, according to Craig, are not determined by actual consequences in the real world: right and wrong come from the decree of the dictator, not from measuring actual harm.

Craig thinks God has a loftier view of what causes harm than we do, so he cannot be judged, but then he goes ahead and judges him:

> Moreover, God had good reason for giving this command. He waited 400 years, while the Israelites were slaves in Egypt, until the Canaanite nation was so wicked, so debauched, that it was ripe for divine judgment. And so he used the armies of Israel as an instrument of his judgment upon these clans in Canaan, knowing ultimately that their extermination would be better for Israel in the long

run—they wouldn't be contaminated by their influences—that these persons were deserving of judgment."

If God can't be judged by human standards, then it shouldn't matter if we think the debauchery of the Canaanites or the genocide of the Israelites is good or evil. If we can't judge God, then it is equally fatuous for us to defend him. It is not up to us to ask for reasons; it is only God who decides. (I'm sure you understand that by talking about "God," I am not agreeing he exists. If I were to say that the Big Bad Wolf is a despicable character, you would know that I am talking about a literary invention, not a real person, who would be bad *if* he existed.) When humans are acting under God's command, according to Craig, then nothing they do can be immoral. If God orders it, the massacre of innocent children is a good and holy act:

> I think the hardest thing to understand is how God could command that even the *children* of the Canaanites be slaughtered. But that's why I say God isn't under moral compulsion to prolong anybody's life. If he wants to strike my son or daughter dead, that's his prerogative, and no moral complaint can be raised about that because God isn't under any moral duty to prolong their life, and so he has the right to take the lives of the Canaanite children or to prolong them as he sees fit. And if he uses the Israeli [sic] army as his instrument by which he does that, then it seems to me he's perfectly within his rights to do that.

"No moral complaint can be raised" about God? Then why does Craig need to defend his god by claiming that those children were murdered for their own good?

> Actually, that's the paradox: the children, by being killed are really, in one sense, better off if we believe children go to heaven, as I do, than

they would be, allowing to live on in the circumstances in which they were.

This is despicable. There is no heaven—and Craig certainly does not know if such a place exists—but even if there were, how does it make killing right? (He actually shoots himself in the foot. Craig's reasoning is a good argument for abortion: kill the fetuses now so they can go to heaven without the risk of being raised in a godless family.) This idiocy of theodicy makes a mockery of morality. Under this kind of thinking, *no* action would be wrong. It puts the lie to the Christian claim of moral absolutes. Nothing that humans value dearly, including the lives of our beloved children, would count for squat. No human is capable of acting morally, which turns into a joke the Christian claim that our moral impulses were implanted by God. If you believe that God commanded you to do something that "in the absence of a divine command" would be obviously atrocious, then is such an act actually good? This is moral bankruptcy, but I know exactly where it comes from. It comes from the purpose-driven life whose goal is to bring glory to God. It comes from the toddler morality of pleasing Daddy. The father figure is always right, *must* be always right (he is the father, after all), and to challenge his goodness will hurt his feelings, offend his ego, undermine his authority, and get you in deep trouble. No matter what he does, Daddy is good—God is good, good, good, they have to keep telling themselves.

Those of us who do not saddle ourselves with such perverse purpose—who are no longer toddlers—are free to say to parents and authority figures: "You did wrong." No one can prevent me from exercising my ethical judgment whenever and however I choose. If I think my Dad or the president or the pope screwed up, I will say so. If I think the god character depicted in the bible acted like a monster, I have the freedom and the right to condemn such actions. To do less would be to abdicate moral responsibility.

Blasphemy is a moral impulse.

Blasphemy is insulting or attributing evil intentions to God, which I just did. It is clear why church leaders would invent such a crime. Blasphemy undermines *their* authority. The old joke that "blasphemy is a victimless crime" doesn't go far enough. Blasphemy is no crime at all. It arises from healthy human judgment. When the Church made blasphemy illegal they were actually acknowledging our natural human ethical impulses and conclusions. When someone accuses me of blasphemy—and this does happen from time to time—I usually reply: "Wow! Thank you for the compliment!" No authoritarian father can tolerate a bratty child who challenges his commands. Biblical morality says: "Shut up and don't ask questions. God is good, good, good, no matter what you think. God said it, I believe it, and that settles it." No matter what crimes he commands or commits, including gross genocide against human families unknowingly trespassing on his holy property, we are to pretend, against all we consider decent and moral, that "God is love."

So, according to William Lane Craig, if a group of people claims that their god granted them a piece of real estate—a Holy Land—that means they automatically have the moral authority to defend their property by any means against anyone they deem to be "evil." Suppose my brothers and I were to return to our tribe's ancestral land of Manahatta (Manhattan), claiming that our ancient Lenape god had given us that land forever and that the invading Big Apple Tribe of foreign squatters is desecrating our holy sites. The Manetta River was one such site, now completely desecrated and covered over, turned into Canal Street. Our ancient trail, which originally followed the high ridge of the island, was broadened into a street of sinfulness. Now marvel in horror at the materialistic debauchery of Broadway! See all the free sex, and paid sex. Look at how our sacred holy drumming site has been turned into Washington Square Park, named in honor of an invading warrior, a place where self-destructive drugs are sold and idolatrous music is performed.[26] Gaze at the shocking display of the pagan god Mercury in Rockefeller Center!

As far as I know, my tribe has never hinted at reclaiming our homeland, but imagine if some Delaware Indian warriors were to threaten to set off nuclear devices in the Theater District, claiming that we were sent by our Lenape Lord, "the only true God," to punish the evildoers and cleanse our divinely inherited land of all that is unholy. Would William Lane Craig judge us? On what grounds? If our Lenape Lord told us to reclaim our "holy land," then Craig, by his own logic, would be grossly out of line for criticizing our actions, even if in the absence of a divine command such actions would look reprehensible. If Craig were to object that our genocidal attack wiped out innocent children, we could simply reply that he, being a fallen non-Lenape human, is incapable of judging our Lenape Lord. It is our solemn duty to follow the orders of the one who issues moral orders. If *you* kill children it is wrong, but if we do it under the command of our Supreme American Lawgiver, then it is not only right, it is a sacred honor and a "moral duty." If you object that the holocaust of entire families and neighborhoods is barbaric, I could smugly inform you that you are not in a position to judge the consequences because you don't know that those children aren't better off being killed—their souls free to flow eternally down the Manetta River under Canal Street—and spared a much worse fate than if they had to sit through an iniquitous Broadway musical. Our God is good, because he told us he is good. New Yorkers are evil because they are offending his holiness and corrupting our tribe. If you judge our Lenape Lord to be evil, then you are committing blasphemy.

That is all very silly. We are intelligent, caring, rational animals who are capable of assessing harm. Based on his violent genocidal behavior (if he existed), we would have a moral right and a duty to judge Lenape Lord to be a Delaware Demon. For the same reasons, I have a right and a responsibility to judge Yahweh, as described in the bible, to be a moral monster.[27] Of course, the real monsters are those people who commit genocide and violence in the name of their imaginary deities, holding up holiness as a mask for violence.

If we can't judge God to be bad, then neither can we judge him to be good. To worship God is to judge God. If what look like "bad" actions of God might actually be good, then what look like "good" actions of God might actually be bad, and we are helpless to know the difference. When he tells us he is good, he might be lying, and if believers think he is not, they are judging him. If they can judge God, why can't I? They say he is good by his decree. I say he is bad by his actions.

Notice that Christianity has an obverse view of morality: in place of instinct, reason, and an evolving humanistic law, it has original sin, faith, and a divinely revealed absolute law. Many Christians preach a tripartite human nature—body, soul, and spirit—which might map crudely to our three "minds." But this framework is doomed to failure since it completely replaces the reason for morality (minimizing harm) with something else, such as following rules or flattering the ego of a dictator whose purpose is to bring glory to himself.

The bible preaches a pessimistic view of human nature. "For all have sinned and come short of the glory of God."[28] There's that intimidating word "glory." Notice that biblical wrongdoing is connected not with real human suffering but with offending the deity. We are all bad: "All have turned away, they have together become worthless; there is no one who does good, not even one."[29] We all deserve to die: "The wages of sin is death."[30] Notice here that death is not viewed as a natural event but as a punishment for the crime of not glorifying the deity. "As in Adam all die, so in Christ shall all be made alive."[31] Without Jesus, we are all doomed. We are all sinners who deserve eternal torment. We are unable to live a good life on our own because we are corrupted with the original sin transmitted to us through Adam. (I never thought of this when I was a preacher, but if "sin" is inherited, is it genetic?)

A humanistic view of human nature is neither negative nor positive. It is realistic and optimistic. We recognize that we all fall somewhere across a spectrum of characteristics and tendencies that are a mix of violence and empathy. Some will lean more toward "saint" and others toward "sinner," but except for a few people at the far end of the curve who are truly mentally unhealthy, most of us are neither wholly "bad" nor wholly "good" by nature. We are wholly human. (I put "bad" and "good" in quotes because they seem to smack of cosmic judgment, not measurable biological traits.) However, even if we aren't wholly "good" by nature, we have the potential to be wholly moral if we make it a priority to act in ways that minimize harm.

Unlike most believers, most humanists are optimistic about human nature. It's not that we think we are perfect, or even perfectible, but that we can improve. Many individual genetic predispositions cannot be changed, or cannot be changed easily, but this does not mean that an individual cannot control his or her own actions in spite of those tendencies. This is where education, societal expectation, and humanistic law become useful.

Many Christians think humanistic optimism is unwarranted. "Just look at the headlines!" they tell us. "The world is in a mess. We are all sinners. We need a savior." Well, yes, look at the headlines. Those are headlines because they are . . . headlines, meant to grab attention. They are unusual. They are shocking. Most of us, fortunately, are somewhere in the middle of the bell curve and live our lives outside of the headlines. Think of a horrible story you have read in the newspaper or seen on television. When a mother does something unthinkable to her children or a husband brutalizes his wife, what do you think? When a criminal commits a heinous act, what do you say? If you are like me, you say, "What an inhuman thing to do!" We assume that those violent acts reported in the headlines do not reflect basic human nature. We know we are normally kind, empathetic, altruistic, loving, and moral, and that is what makes headlines grab our attention. It is good that most people don't make it to those headlines. It is only the extreme deviations from the norm that catch our attention, and they shock us because they are *not* representative of who we really are.

Often we hear sermons announcing that without God we would all be horrible people, stealing, raping, killing, lying. Human nature is hopelessly corrupt. But is it really? If you are a believer, is that how you picture yourself? Are you desperately trying to restrain your malicious impulses? If you could get away with it, would you run around like a maniac, looting, destroying property, sexually assaulting, and causing bodily harm? Don't you simply *know* that such behavior is a threat to survival? Most human beings who want a good life prefer less violence, less harm. Studies show that societies with less religion are better off,[32] so there must be a tendency to a natural goodness that is not in need of divine correction. Since harm is something we biologically want to avoid, most of us are naturally moral. In that sense, I think we can say we are born with "original good" rather than "original sin."

Sure, you can probably picture yourself acting violently. Each one of us, if pressed hard enough, could be prompted to hurt others. Even the gentlest mother might become a screaming attacker if her children were threatened by a child rapist or murderer. It's not that she desires to cause harm to others but that she might have to, to save her children. Self-defense is morally defensible. If your intention is to minimize harm, then you might sometimes have to cause some harm to accomplish that (regrettably or not). I suppose that is part of the equation in the debate to engage in a "just war," if such a concept is meaningful or workable. Even the most ardent pacifists will call the police if there is an intruder in their house, hoping the authorities will arrive with enough show of force to neutralize the threat. Violence is part of the arsenal of survival mechanisms available to us, inherited from our ancestors who managed to escape death long enough to breed and nurture their offspring. But in general, most of us want a life of peace and safety and only view violence as a sometimes unfortunate necessary defensive action, not as a way of life.

Mere Morality is the preference for a world with less harm. Sometimes it is hard to spot the harm in a situation. Is it wrong to cheat on a test? At face value, it would seem that if you can get away with it, cheating on a test hurts no one and gives you a better chance at success in life. But with a little thought the harm becomes clear. If the class is graded on a curve, then by artificially boosting your GPA you have lowered everyone else's, perhaps dropping another student's grade from one level to another. This difference might be enough to cause that other student to someday lose getting a job when an employer is comparing GPAs on resumes, and that could materially affect their earning potential and their quality of life. On its face, unfairness sometimes doesn't seem to cause much harm, but the consequences in the long run can be significant. If the class is not graded on a curve, there is still the fact that your own GPA becomes inflated, making you appear more qualified to a future employer than you actually are, perhaps causing them to pass by a better candidate for the job. This can affect the profitability of that company, impacting all other employees, harming their lives as a result. If your profession deals with public safety, such as architecture, engineering, or medicine, then the fact that you are overrated can be a real danger to society. If you are the kind of person who cheats on a test, you may also cheat on the job, opening yourself to the possibility of malpractice. (My daughter Sabrina suggested another possible harm from cheating. The professor might alter the test if the curve shifts artificially, causing the next class to find it harder to get a good grade.)

Look for the harm and you will understand morality.

The harm principle is a moral minimum, a *mere* morality that can be shared by all of us. If you happen to be a compassionate and loving person, then you will go beyond Mere Morality, beyond simply minimizing harm, and actively work to enhance the lives of others. Charity is admirable, and the world would certainly be worse off if none of us practiced it, but I don't think there is a charity imperative like there is a moral imperative. Charity beyond the moral minimum should be encouraged, but not expected of everyone. (I happen to think universal health care is a moral minimum, and a country that refuses it should be ashamed of itself.) If you simply avoid causing unnecessary harm, you are passively moral—"merely moral." If you choose to go further by giving, sacrificing, volunteering, and proactively investing in the well-being and improvement of the lives of others, then you are displaying a character that is truly useful and admirable, and we value you precisely *because* you are going above and beyond the minimum morality. It is a choice, not an imperative—if it were expected or demanded, it would not be praiseworthy. The fact that many of us choose to be compassionate, helpful, and charitable is a mark of distinction of which our species can be proud. It is part of what makes humanity beautiful.

Mere Morality cannot determine in advance what is the right behavior in every case. That would turn it into a lifeless formula. We have to figure it out on our own, depending on the situation. All moral decisions are situational: they need to be evaluated by the context, not by hard-and-fast rules. For example, telling a lie is usually harmful, but sometimes it is the right thing to do.

My friend Buzz Kemper, a sound engineer who co-owns the Audio For the Arts recording studio and who is the announcer for Freethought Radio, told me a story about a quick decision he had to make while mountain climbing. Buzz is an experienced climber, having completed ascents as difficult as F5.11, and scaled Devil's Tower numerous times. He was climbing one day with his friend "Bear," who was sometimes a bit skittish, as all of us would be, and had an instinctive tendency to freeze up in fear when things got difficult or dangerous. Buzz was below and Bear was near the top of a moderately difficult ascent when the rope became unsecure and Bear sensed that something might be wrong. "Is everything okay?" he called down. Buzz immediately knew that everything was not okay, that his friend was lacking protection, and that they were both in serious danger if he slipped, but he also knew that the remaining short distance to the top was not difficult, so he quickly replied, "Yes, everything is fine. Go ahead." Bear easily scrambled up the rest of the way and waited for Buzz to follow. "It just so happens that I know how his mind works," Buzz said. "While I knew he was more than capable of completing that route if he stayed calm, I also knew that telling him the truth about the situation would have psyched him out, as it would have for me had our positions been reversed." When Buzz got to the top, he told Bear what had happened and admitted that he had lied to him. After a moment's thought, his friend replied, "Thank you. You did the right thing." So far, everyone who has heard this story has agreed with Buzz that telling a lie was the moral thing to do. If he had told the truth, they would have both been at greater risk.

There are no simplistic rules. Life is often messy, and to find the path that is the most moral we usually have to juggle our three "moral minds," hoping to arrive at some clarity, or at least a justification for why we think a certain action results in less harm than another. If you recognize that instinct, reason, and humanistic law are useful guides, and then test the results against actual harm, then you are a good person. A good Christian. A good Jew, Hindu, Buddhist, or Muslim. A good atheist. A good human being.

Real ethical dilemmas arise when there is a conflict among our three moral minds. When reason tells you to do something that instinct tells you to avoid, you are at war with yourself. Whatever you do in such a situation is either going to feel bad or appear bad, even if it is the right thing to do. When instinct or reason points you to do something that is against the law, you are at war with society. Sometimes there is no "right" answer. Sometimes we just have to live with who we are and can console ourselves that at least we are doing our best trying to minimize harm.

One of the hypothetical moral dilemmas given in Philosophy 101 classes involves a burning building with children trapped inside. Behind one door are ten screaming kids, and behind the other door is one desperate child. You only have the time or the ability to open one of the doors. Which one do you choose? I think we all agree that reason will direct us to the door with ten children. It would be a horrible choice, knowing that such a decision results in the death of that one child who could have been saved if you had chosen otherwise. But ten is more than one, and based on the principle of minimizing harm, you are justified in rationally directing your action toward the larger group of children, even though you feel a massive reluctance and sorrow at abandoning the one child to its death. No one could fault you for such a decision, and even though you would feel anguished, you should not punish yourself.

Now add one fact to the situation and see if you would act differently. Suppose you realized that the one child was your own. All eleven kids are screaming, but your own is calling "Mommy!" or "Daddy!" How would that affect your rational calculations? I am pretty sure you are just like me: you would save your own child first. Rationally it would appear wrong, but instinctively and "morally" it would be right. None of the parents of the other children, though angry and grieving, would fault your decision because they know that they would have done the same thing. Parenting instincts are extremely powerful. Not only are we genetically closer to our children (giving us the evolutionary justification for protecting our own inheritance), but we know our kids. We love them and they love us. We have spent years with them, singing them lullabies, putting bandages on their scratches, tending to their needs. We know that our own children have come to depend on our personal promise to take care of them. We have looked in their eyes and promised that we will always love and protect them. I challenge you to pretend that you could ignore such a powerful evolutionary tendency to protect your own offspring by mechanically rushing to save the other children first. Parenting is a natural responsibility, after all, that all families recognize and respect.

Even if it were a hundred children, I would still feel the pull of my own child stronger than the others. But I suppose it is possible that if the number were great enough, and if there were enough time to think about it, I would have to consider violating my own instincts and breaking my promise to my own child in order to save the lives of so many others. This would make some evolutionary sense as well, since we all share common genes, and those other children are in my species, and even though I love my own children more, I don't hate any of those other kids. If I were ever forced into making such a decision, I might steel myself and choose the rationally "right" action knowing that it was the instinctively "wrong" action. Under the mental anguish of such a decision, I might then be tempted to end my own life in order to avoid living on with the loss of my own child, hating myself for such a betrayal (and I hope you would try to prevent me from doing that). A parenting instinct is a lens that magnifies the worth of, hence the risk of harm to, our own offspring. Taking everything into account, a moral action is one that intends to minimize harm, sometimes in line with our natural feelings and sometimes in spite of them.

One example of an ethical thought experiment that seems to stump or surprise people is the Trolley Problem.[33] It is indeed an intriguing moral conundrum, but I think the "answer" is in the fact that reason and instinct are in conflict. I put "answer" in quotes because I don't think there is a correct decision to the dilemma; I think there is a good reason why there is no correct decision.

The basic Trolley Problem goes like this. A runaway trolley is hurtling down the tracks. Ahead, there are five people tied up on the tracks, unable to move out of the way. You are standing by the switch that can divert the train to a different track, but you notice that there is one person tied up on the side track. If you do nothing, five people die. If you move the switch, one person will die. What should you do?

Using reason—the harm principle—most people say they would move the switch. One person is less than five, and that would be the least amount of overall harm. (Some of those who say they would not move the switch think they can avoid moral responsibility by not getting involved, but I think not acting would be just as much a moral choice as acting.) Using rational calculation alone, moving the switch seems to be the correct answer, the lesser of two evils. I would feel horrible with either decision, but at least I could give a reason for my choice to move the switch.

So far, that is not so difficult. A paradox occurs, however, when the same problem is cast in a different scenario. The same trolley is heading for five people, but this time you are standing on a bridge under which the trolley must pass before hitting the people. An enormously heavy man is standing on the bridge next to you, and you realize that if you push him off, he will stop the trolley and be killed, and you will save the lives of the five people. What do you do?

It seems that using reason—the harm principle—there is no difference between the two scenarios, but most people say they would *not* push the heavy man onto the tracks. Why not? Both scenarios involve taking action to minimize harm. Are the five people less deserving this time? Is the heavy man more deserving than the one tied up on the tracks? Why is one action correct while the equivalent action is incorrect?

I think this is because although the consequences are identical, the actions are not. In the first scenario, although you feel horrible, the one man killed is not so close to you. In the second scenario, you have to physically touch the man and cause his death in a more direct manner. You can't really look away. You are more likely to look in his eyes. He is more likely to communicate fear and disappointment. Your biological instincts toward preserving life are stronger when you are closer to the person. It is more difficult to separate yourself from the harm you are committing (in order to minimize greater harm) when there is nothing separating you from the physical act, such as a mechanical switch. The same kind of instinct that caused me to reach for the falling baby, with no conscious thought, would also cause me to feel revulsion at deliberately causing another human being to fall to his death. The same kind of instinct that causes you to save the life of your own child over the lives of ten children in the burning building would also cause you to feel a kind of moral obligation to the person into whose eyes you are looking. I'm not saying either decision is ethically correct—to push or not to push—I'm just saying that if you don't push the overweight man onto the tracks, you have a good instinctively moral justification, if not a coldly calculated reason. You probably can't help acting compassionately toward the person in whose eyes you are looking. We wouldn't blame the heavy man himself for not voluntarily jumping, so why should we blame you for not pushing him?

Ethical thought experiments with no clear answer are disturbing, but fortunately, we don't live our lives in such distressing hypothetical emergencies. If we did, we would all have heart attacks and the species would die out. I think the reason we are uncomfortable with ethical dilemmas is because we think there always *must* be a correct answer. Life doesn't always offer a "correct" answer, and the best we can often do is intend to head in the right direction, away from harm, however we perceive it. I think this whole discussion actually underscores the fact that by nature, we are instinctively good animals who are trying our best.

Mere Morality can be summarized as: using instinct, law, and reason as guides, try to act with the intention of minimizing harm.

When you are confronting a moral decision, first consider how you feel about it. Often, you will simply know what to do, by instinct. I knew I should catch that falling baby even before I knew it. But ancestral impulses can also be wrong in a novel situation, especially in an environment different from the one in which the instinct evolved.

Second, remind yourself what the law says, if anything, about the actions you are contemplating. Many moral dilemmas have nothing to do with the law, but when they do, your society is talking to you. If a law is concerned with minimizing real harm, then it is a good law. If not, you can morally ignore it, although you might have to suffer the legal penalties until you can get that bad law overturned.

Third, and most important, use reason to think it through. Reason may contradict instinct and law that, followed blindly, might cause more harm in a particular situation. Try to be as informed as you can about the results of your actions so that you can weigh the consequences and pick the path that leads to the least amount of overall harm.

And fourth—this is not a moral mind or ethical imperative, but an additional option, a dessert—after having done all of the above, you are welcome to go beyond the ethical minimum of Mere Morality and invest in the lives of others through charity, volunteerism, and compassionate actions. Charity is not an imperative for morality any more than art or music are requirements for society, but it is nice that there are so many individuals—and these include millions of good atheists—who do choose to go beyond Mere Morality to try to make this a planet with less violence, more understanding, more beauty, and more happiness.

I smiled when I first heard the question: "If the purpose of life is to make others happy, what is *their* purpose of life?" Helping to make others happy is a good thing, but it is not the purpose of life. Happiness is not something you lack until someone else gives it to you. It's a state of contentment that includes having your basic needs met, sensing you are out of danger, and feeling that you are free to do what you need or want to do. If you can't be happy knowing that others are not, then you are empathetic, and working to lessen the unhappiness of others gives you some purpose in your life. But it is not "the purpose of life." Somewhere, somehow, somebody has to *be* happy, and that is an end in itself. Why shouldn't that somebody be you? And since everybody is a "you," why can't we all strive to be happy and help others to be happy?

My Mom used to say, "If you want to be happy, then be happy." She knew it wasn't that simple, but we understood what she meant. She was almost always singing, humming, smiling, maybe a bit Pollyannaish, but we loved her. She was fun. She knew that we have a lot of control over our decisions, so why not be optimistic? She thought happiness was something we can choose to feel, and maybe that is not true for everybody, but I think we *can* say that about our actions. We can choose to be moral. Instead of making morality a huge mystery, searching for an "absolute standard" or list of rules or external ethical imperative or purpose-driven motivation or other excuse to treat people nicely, why not simply choose to be reasonable, moral, and kind to others? Paraphrasing my Mom: "If you want to be a good person, then be a good person."

3

RELIGIOUS COLOR BLINDNESS

Annie Laurie has a small knit hat that she wears during the cooler months, and she is very attached to it. Well, it could be better attached, because she keeps losing it. But like a cat, the hat keeps coming back with another life. I once found it in our driveway. It was missing for a whole week last winter, and when we went to the radio station to record another episode of Freethought Radio, Annie Laurie asked Lisa, the receptionist, if anyone might have spotted a small puce hat.

"Oh, I might have seen something like that in the bushes by the parking lot," Lisa said. Annie Laurie must have dropped it getting into the car the week before. It had stormed in the meantime, and the hat must have blown across the parking lot. Lisa took her to the spot, where she dug the hat out of the snow, to Annie Laurie's surprise and relief.

A couple of months later she lost the hat again, sometime between a lunch visit with her mother and later that evening when we both returned to her mother's independent-living apartment to play Scrabble. As we were leaving the building that night, Annie Laurie was lamenting the loss of her favorite hat. "I asked at the front desk if anyone has seen a small puce hat, and nobody has." The moment she said that, I pointed to a small object someone had placed on the ledge she had walked past just outside the building.

"That's it!" she said. "How many lives does my hat have?"

A small *puce* hat?

The word "puce" has never crossed my lips. It has never crossed my mind, until now. I see it as a kinda darkish hat, and if I were forced to describe it, I would say it is dull purple, maybe a dusty plum color, though I don't think I have ever said the word "plum" as a color. In my mind, that hat is just "a color," I don't know. I am surprised not only that Annie Laurie would find a word for it, but that others would know what she means.

It is no secret that Annie Laurie has a finer sense of color and style than I do. Maybe it is a girl/guy thing, but I do hear men talking like her. I am impressed when fashion designers, interior decorators, and artists speak about their craft.

In college, I went on a date with a student named Patty. When I showed up at her dorm room, she opened the door, looked at me, and said, "I'm not going out with you like that!"

I looked at my clothes and said, "What?" Having dressed up for the evening, I was wearing burgundy polyester slacks and a bright-red long-sleeved dress shirt.

"Those colors are horrible!" she said. "Go back and change."

I slunk back to my dorm room, now acutely self-conscious, entering the building through the back door instead of the front where I had just exited in full view of the world. My face probably matched my clothes. I still have trouble locating the word "burgundy" in my brain, as a color. The shirt was maybe scarlet, cardinal, or tomato, but all I can remember is red. Never mind that even if the pants and shirt *had* matched, that would not have been exactly classy.

I do often need Annie Laurie's fashion advice. Sometimes I protest that I'm just way ahead of the times for her, but I have to concede she is usually right when it comes to color and style.

On the other hand, I have a highly fine-tuned sense of music. Pun intended. Like an aural fashion designer, I can usually tell you exactly what is happening in a piece of music and why it is beautiful. It's not just mechanical training. Those harmonies are like colors, not that I see actual colors, but that I identify the chords, progressions, modes, and relations of the melodic notes in a "musically knowing" way. (I did once "see" music in color, one Saturday morning in a hypnopompic state as I was gradually awakened by a music alarm radio. It was wonderful, but only lasted about a minute. I have always wished I could repeat that experience.)

I hear the chords by feeling them, much like we sense colors. Other jazz players tell me I have a great ear. Now, make yourself read the rest of this paragraph, even if you don't follow it. I can immediately "see" the IV chord (subdominant), the II chord (dominant of the dominant, if major), a sharp eleven on a dominant seventh, a flatted ninth on the III-7 chord (mediant), a subtonic with the fifth in the bass, a minor chord with a major seventh, the sharp 6th of the Dorian and sharp 4th of the Lydian mode, the 13th as a melodic passing or neighboring tone between 5 and 7—and so on, with hundreds of subtle combinations effortlessly "visible" to my ear. I don't have to state those exact words while hearing the music, any more than you have to describe the precise grammar while reading a sentence, although you could if you wanted to. I can hear/feel the counterpoint of the bass line. (If there is a next life, I will come back as a bassist.) And after all that—if the music is not too "out there" or atonal—I can usually place or transpose that into any one of the twelve tonalities, a skill that many singers appreciate when they ask me to play in a different key to fit their voice.

If that paragraph seems opaque or pretentious to you, then you know how I feel when people talk about fashion. When I say those things to Annie Laurie, she sometimes shrugs, as I sometimes roll my eyes when she asks for my opinion about an outfit she is considering purchasing.

Of course, Annie Laurie hears what I hear, and I see what she sees, so neither of us is missing anything. She enjoys music no less than I do. She is not deaf, and I am not blind. We are just attuned in different ways. We "see" the world differently. We have given ourselves a vocabulary for what we perceive. I hear the dominant seventh and she sees puce.

I would guess that most of the difference comes from culture and training, but certainly some of it is due to genetic variation. Some scientists suspect there are a few women who were born with four-color cones in their retinas instead of the usual three cones. They can perceive hundreds more shades and combinations of colors. Maybe they are seeing fifty shades of puce.

I am not a wine drinker. I am not a drinker at all. Maybe twice a year Annie Laurie and I will share a glass of champagne, as a symbolic celebration of an event. On the few occasions I have sipped wine, it tastes like, well, like wine. I can't discriminate. What does bouquet or balanced taste mean? How can wine be brilliant or broad, flowery or noble? What is the difference between spicy and fruity? I'm sure those words mean something special to connoisseurs and that I am missing out on a very real enjoyment in life. Scott, the webmaster at the Freedom From Religion Foundation, is a beer/ale expert who knows all the microbreweries in the area (and many around the world) and can describe hundreds of different tastes with precise explanations. To me, beer is beer. (Well, the first and only glass I had was more than thirty years ago.) Am I "taste blind"? The only thing wine does is put me to sleep.

Human characteristics vary across the population. Even without training, some people naturally have a better sense of style, color, taste, smell, and music. Same with sports, math, language, science, engineering, and all other activities in our species. Each of us falls somewhere on the bell curve of variety. But even if there is nothing wrong with our brains or my senses—even if we have no genetic or pathological defects—we can still be "brain blind."

Cultural Color Blindness

In his book *Antifragile*, Nassim Nicholas Taleb distinguishes between genetic color blindness and "cultural color blindness." Genetic color blindness is a physical disability. Cultural color blindness is a lack of names for the finer shades of light frequency that we do not recognize.

The ancient Greeks, Taleb tells us, did not have the word "blue." William Gladstone, the former prime minister of England, did an exhaustive analysis of Homer's writings and discovered that they were pale by comparison with later literature, with less color words than modern writings. Homer called the sea "wine dark." The Greeks saw blue, of course, but they didn't "see" blue—just like I don't "see" puce. They didn't give it a name. Some cultures do not identify all colors, or the same colors, with names. Linguist Guy Deutscher notices that in the evolution of language, blue is always the last color to be named.

Linguist Daniel Everett, in his book *Don't Sleep, There Are Snakes*—in which he tells his story of being a missionary to the Pirahã tribe in the Amazon only to end up being converted to atheism like his happy hosts—describes the Pirahã language as lacking names for colors. Instead of green, they say "like a leaf." We do the same in English with words like "orange," "peach," and "cherry" for particular colors or shades, but for us those are names. For the Pirahã, they are descriptions. They don't have words for even the basic colors of yellow, red, green, or blue.

Blue is at the faster end (shorter wave length) of the spectrum of light visible to humans. Red, on the other end, is slower (hence the famous redshift of light as stars move away from us), with a wavelength about twice as long. Perhaps blue, being small and swift, is tougher for the cones in our retinas to handle, or more likely to be filtered out as parts of the eye degrade when we age.

My Granddad Barker, a member of the Delaware Indian (Lenape) tribe, had trouble with blue when he aged. I sometimes watched him as he labored over his loom creating native beadwork, often humming a melody from his childhood. Grandma, who was quarter Cherokee, had to keep reorganizing his beads in little plastic boxes because he would often get them mixed up. I have a hatband he made for me—a zigzag blue river with a red border on a white background—and right in the middle of the river is a naughty green bead. That hatband has real sentimental value for me. I *love* that little mistake—that's my Granddad! (It is getting harder for me to spot that lone bead, so what does that tell you about *my* eyes?)

Neurologist Oliver Sacks, in his book *Island of the Colorblind*, describes a whole group of people who live in a black-and-white world. They are physically unable to see color.

But genetic or aging defects wouldn't explain why an entire civilization would lack words for certain colors. I think Taleb is right when he suggests that culture and training can fine-tune our attentiveness, helping us "see" what we see, just like I am trying to learn that not all reds go together.

It's not just vision. We also sometimes don't "hear" what we hear. On a recent episode of Freethought Radio, I introduced our guest, whose name is Dawn.

"You mean Dawn," Annie Laurie interrupted, "not Don."

"That's what I said," I replied, not hearing the difference.

It turns out that this is a regional variation. I was born and raised in California, and Annie Laurie is from the Midwest. Dawn, our guest on that show, confirmed that there is a difference. Originally from Chicago, where she said her name with the deeper "aw" sound, she has since moved to Oregon where most people call her "Don." Those two women can hear the difference, and I suppose I can too, but I don't hear two distinct vowels. I hear regional accents of the same sound. On the other hand, Annie Laurie pronounces Oregon like "Oregawn" instead of "Oregun," as they say it in the state. The city of Oregon, Wisconsin, is indeed pronounced like Annie Laurie says it. I have to admit that Annie Laurie's perception of that vowel sound is more refined than mine. But you should hear how she tries to pronounce Spanish, not hearing the shades of "d" or "b," or the pure sound of "e."

When I was learning Spanish in high school, I could not roll the letter "R" like my Hispanic friends could. I really wanted to master the language, so I spent months forcing myself to mechanically spit and stutter the letter. I remember many hours riding my bike around town, repeating the exercise, "Rr con rr cigarros. Rr con rr barril. Rápido ruedan las ruedas de los carros del ferrocarril." At first I was just mangling my tongue, but eventually I got it, and it now rolls easily. On the other hand, many of my Hispanic friends have trouble with English vowels. The sentence, "Ship a cheap sheep chip," sounds like repeating the same word to them.

I suppose our other senses are the same. Blind people report "seeing" the world through touch. Individuals certainly have different sensitivities of smell and taste.

I happen to have a rare and harmless condition called synesthesia. I see all letters and numbers in color. Most are blue, green, red, yellow, orange, and brown, though a few are black and gray, and a couple are shades of white. Some are different variants of the same color. "R" and "M" are green, but "R" is brighter, more sparkly. The letter "V" is a color that does not exist in reality, a kind of purple-brown—not like puce—sort of like a shiny copper penny with a violet reflection. But when I say that I "see" them, I don't mean they actually change color on the page. Those colors are in the mind, in the same way that you "see" a yellow banana in a black-and-white movie.

So the human mind can see things it doesn't see, and not see things it does see. This might explain much of what goes on with religion.

Religious Color Blindness

I think cultural color blindness is evident in religion. When I talk about my journey from evangelical preacher to atheist, I often say that fundamentalists have binary brains. Not all believers are that extreme, of course, but all fundamentalists are absolutists. To the righteous mind, there is no middle ground. Everything is right or wrong, true or false, good or evil. Jesus reportedly said, "I wish you were cold or hot. So then because you are lukewarm, and neither cold nor hot, I will spew you out of my mouth." To the true believer, there is no warmth, no gray area. It is all black and white.

But now I think I can say it better: fundamentalists have polarized brains. The difference between black and white is not gray: it is a color spectrum. Their world is monochromatic, not black-and-white. They don't perceive the rich colors of life within the rainbow.

The prophet Jeremiah complained that there are "foolish people, and without understanding; which have eyes, and see not; which have ears, and hear not." Jesus reportedly said, "Having eyes do you not see, and having ears do you not hear?" They admit that it is possible to perceive without perceiving, but I think they were writing about themselves. They are the ones who are spewing distasteful colors out of their mouths.

Think about sexuality. The bible says that "God created mankind in his own image, in the image of God he created them; male and female he created them" (Genesis 1:27). It is assumed that Adam and Eve were heterosexual, because they were commanded to "replenish the earth." Jesus made the same assumption: "Have you not read that He who created them from the beginning made them male and female, and said 'for this reason a man shall leave his father and mother and be joined to his wife, and the two shall become one flesh'?" (This is also sexist, from the male point of view.) In the bible, anything outside of binary heterosexuality is condemned as an abomination. (See Leviticus 20:13, for example.)

To fundamentalist bible believers, there are only two sexual identities: men who love women, and women who love men. It's not that they don't know there are alternative sexual practices; they just don't see them for what they are: varieties, or colors, in a spectrum of sexual inclinations. Just like in my mind there is no difference between "Dawn" and "Don," to the fundamentalist, there is no such thing as a gay, lesbian, bisexual, or transgender person. People with alternate lifestyles are just different accents, or deviations of heterosexuals. Hence, they are deviant. They are "straights" who are crooked. Everybody must be biblically polarized, socially shoehorned into one-size-fits-all. Any identity that does not flip to one side of their toggle switch does not exist. This is a cultural color blindness resulting from religion, a failure to see the shades of reality we are looking at. Forcing homosexuals to live as heterosexuals is like me pretending that my garish red outfit was attractive. It is fitting that the gay community uses a rainbow as a symbol.

Think about geology. Instead of seeing the various strata at the Grand Canyon as revealing different ages in a history spanning billions of years, young-earth creationists are forced to view all the layers as instantly created on the first of six days of creation. The canyon was carved in less than forty days in a worldwide flood, they insist, instead of over about six million years. This is a different kind of flat-earth mentality. While modern geologists are able to tease out the ages of the rocks—the colors in the prism, so to speak—by looking at fossils and using other dating techniques, true believers are wed to a single creative event, allowing only an insignificant amount of change through sedimentation and erosion since the beginning of the world a few thousand years ago. The "Rock of Ages" erases the ages of rocks. They have eyes, and see not.

Think about evolution. The bible says, "God made the beasts of the earth after their kind," and creationists interpret this to mean each species was formed independently. All of life is flat, started at the same moment, existing side-by-side, nothing related. How boring! When you can learn to see the beauty of evolution, the interconnectedness of all living things springing from the same ancestor, it opens up a whole four-dimensional spectrum. We can see ourselves in stereo, in context, as cousins to the other apes, as more distant relatives to every other species on the planet. Viewing biology as different shades within a larger biosphere transforms the pale two-dimensional flat-earth view of one-off specially created species into a wonderful multicolored sphere of interrelated organisms, a true "family of life." When Darwin introduced us to evolution by natural selection, it was like giving new color names to what we were seeing but not seeing. It truly opened our minds. Of course, creationists have heard about fossils, biogeography, homology, and comparative genetics, but having ears to hear, they hear not.

A similar stereo effect happened to me when I went to Brazil. Knowing Spanish, I had a head start learning Portuguese because the two languages are descended from a common ancestor. I might be almost half fluent in Brazilian Portuguese now, though they tell me I have a Mexican accent. I *love* the voices of Bossa Nova and Samba singers—you can sail a ship through those Amazon-wide vowels—and I'm afraid I will never sound like that. But as far as the language goes, I find it fascinating to be looking at two cousins descended from their Latin grandparent, spotting the similarities and the differences.

A light turned on when I learned that the Portuguese word for "almost" is *quasi*. Of course, since we use "quasi-" in English, I can see that it comes from the Latin. But it surprised me when I realized that the Spanish word *casi* is from the same root. All these years I have been saying *casi* as if it were a stand-alone "special creation" from the Spanish language, not seeing the connection. Now with the binocular vision from the related species of Portuguese, I can see the family resemblance, the common ancestor, and the descent with variation. This is just like "seeing" that the human race is not a stand-alone species but a cousin to the other apes, all showing descent with modification. It is a real enhancement when what was two-dimensional comes alive, when a cartoon becomes flesh and blood, when gray scale changes to color, when painting turns to sculpture, when mono turns to stereo, when light turns to prism.

Richard Dawkins, in *The Extended Phenotype*, talks about this shift in perspective as we look at the natural world. He compares it to staring at a drawing of a Necker Cube, where your mind sees a box in one orientation and then surprisingly shifts to the other orientation. Nothing actually changes on the paper—it all happens in your mind—but it feels like something has changed. Two people can be looking at the same facts but "seeing" something entirely different. Fundamentalist creationists perceive a two-dimensional drawing with little depth or meaning, while evolutionary biologists see a three-dimensional image, actually four-dimensional when you consider time.

Think about abortion. Fundamentalist "pro-lifers" view an individual person like they view an individual species, with no evolution leading up to its creation. A human being, like the human race, appears on the stage as a full person, they imagine. Adam was formed as a grown man, not a boy, child, baby, or fetus. To the true believer, there is no such thing as a half-developed person, just like there can be no half-soul. It is black or white, absolute, colorless. While the gestating human actually moves through a spectrum of developmental stages—in many of which the human is indistinguishable from other mammals—the religious anti-abortionists view the whole scenario not as a process but as an instantly completed creation, all involving a fully human person. The sperm contacts the egg and Presto, "You" are created. A zygote, blastocyst, embryo, or fetus is the same as a breathing baby in their polarized brains.

But the rest of us, including many cultures not hampered by a misogynist faith, are able to understand that personhood is not a thing that begins at conception. It arrives somewhere later in the growth of a human organism. An embryo is not a person. A stem cell is not a person. As comedian Bill Maher pointed out in one of his hilarious monologues,[1] you can freeze a stem cell indefinitely, which is something you definitely cannot do with a baby. Even the bible, which equates life with breath, actually seems to agree with modern American law, which acknowledges that a human life begins at viability. I don't know of any fundamentalists who add nine months to their age. But many believers, being religiously colorblind, can only conceive of "life" (a full person) as black or white, red or blue, all or nothing. Those of us who affirm a woman's freedom to decide her own reproductive future equate a human life with personhood, seeing the earlier stages of development within a spectrum leading up to a precious baby whose arrival and existence we do cherish. Personhood is blue, while a zygote is red, with a prism in the middle.

Think about Christianity itself. It is certainly not monochromatic. Even in the early years, there were different flavors of churches and theologies. The early Gnostics, who may have been the first Christians and whose footprints we see in the Logos in the opening verse of the Gospel of John, were not the same as the Ebionites, the Marcionites, or the Pauline Christians. When Constantine came along in the fourth century and crudely hacked Christianity into an official shape by the force of state violence, he polarized the religion into orthodox and unorthodox, black and white, red and blue, insiders and outsiders, "cold or hot." That began a long period of history often called the Dark Ages, a fitting name for color blindness, a coerced conformity to established dogma and ritual.

It wasn't until more than a millennium later that the Enlightenment—another appropriate name—began to tease out scientific truth from dogma. Isaac Newton, one of the early Enlightenment thinkers, is the person who actually taught us about the properties of light, showing that white light is really a combination of the rainbow colors that represent different frequencies of electromagnetic radiation. That momentous revelation was preceded by a similar "unweaving of the rainbow" within the church itself, the Protestant Reformation. The One True Faith splintered into many smaller faiths, an astonishing prism of colors—denominations and theologies—emanating from the Protestant kaleidoscope.

When I left Christianity, it wasn't a sudden giant leap from fundamentalism to atheism. I first moved through a period of migration across that Protestant spectrum (Catholics also now have a spectrum, though not as wide), taking four or five years, starting at the extreme red side of evangelical absolutism and gradually adjusting my views, little by little, liberal by liberal, until I moved to the blue side. I realized early in that process that there is no one Christianity. There may be as many Christianities as there are Christians. Of course, I didn't park my thoughts at the liberal blue side of the Protestant continuum. I like to say that I threw out all the bath water and found there is no baby there. But another way to picture it is that I moved from red through orange, yellow, green, to blue and violet (and maybe puce), finally stepping away from the individual stripes, jumping out of the rainbow into the fullness of white light—Enlightenment—where I can look back and see the prism for what it is. If you are in the rainbow, you can't see the rainbow. Every color in the faith—especially near the slower red frequencies—thinks it is light while the others are dark. They are religiously colorblind.

Think about comparative religion. Once when I was debating a young-earth creationist, I began my opening statement like this:

> In the beginning was the Turtle. The Turtle was swimming across an endless body of water. One day it dove to the bottom and brought up a lump of mud. When the mud baked in the sun, it became dry land. The land expanded into a vast area where trees grew. One day the Rabbit started kicking a blood clot by one of the trees until it formed into a human being.

I explained that this is one version of a Native American creation myth, not unlike some of the tales told by my own Lenape ancestors. (My family is from the Turtle Clan of the tribe.) Humans were telling similar stories on the American continent 12,000 to 15,000 years ago, which, if you believe my opponent, was 9,000 years before the earth was created. I told the audience that I thought that was a charming and enjoyable story, and they nodded.

"How many of you think there really was a Turtle at the beginning?" I asked. No hands went up.

Then I asked how many believed the creation myth of a later group of people, the Bronze Age Israelites, including the earth being created from a watery void, Adam being formed from the mud, Eve being taken from his rib, a talking snake, a talking donkey, a jealous genocidal war god named Yahweh ("my name is Jealous"), the Nile River turning to blood, and food falling from the sky. Most of the hands went up in that audience. They think the Turtle is false but the talking snake is true. They are polarized. They can't see outside their own color.

All human groups have invented meaningful fables, but *their* fable is actual truth, they proclaim. The vast array of colorful creation myths collapses into "us versus them." Truth versus lies. Some believers do appreciate the varieties of religious belief in anthropology; they just see them all as quaint but false, "out there," while *their* belief is the one true faith. They can't see themselves as part of the fabric, or their color as part of a spectrum, or their religion as having evolved from earlier antecedents. In the previous chapter, I talked about how law has ancestors, but the same is true with religion. If you can step back and see that your religion is just one cousin from a grandparent (as Christianity and Islam are descended mainly from Judaism), and also realize that the grandparent is a cousin to other religions descended from even earlier ancestors, you can perceive your faith not as a blunt stand-alone creation, but as a small part of a larger array. Your worldview becomes enriched. Gregory Riley does a nice job of illustrating the family tree (or branching river system) of world faiths in his book *The River of God.*[2]

Former minister John Loftus suggests that the way to gain perspective, to think outside the box, is to take the "outsider test."[3] Look at your own religion as an outsider might see it. Look at your own beliefs the same way you look at the beliefs of others: from a distance. If you can't do that, you are religiously colorblind.

Think about ethics. Most of us, including believers, act as if we embrace situational ethics in our daily lives, but most religions teach that there are absolute moral laws that must be followed no matter what, by command of a dictator. For example, since the Ten Commandments prohibit bearing "false witness" against a neighbor, most Christians think it is always wrong to tell a lie. Not just wrong, but sinful—a character flaw. However, while it is true that honesty is generally a good principle for social harmony, telling a lie is not always immoral. We do have laws against perjury, false advertising, contractual misrepresentation, impersonating an officer, identity theft, and so on, but it is generally not illegal to tell a lie.

Suppose a woman came to your front door, bruised and bleeding, saying that her husband is trying to kill her. You take her into your home, tend to her wounds, give her a place to stay for a while. Later, her husband comes banging on your door, shouting, "Do you know where my wife is?!" What do you do? As a good moral person, do you tell him the truth? I think all of us know that in that particular situation, the most moral thing to do is lie to that man. Otherwise, we risk greater harm to the woman. Telling that lie is not a sin: it is a good act of which you should be proud. But some Christians have told me that although they would indeed lie to the husband, they would feel bad about it and would later ask God for forgiveness. In their polarized brains, telling a lie is always sinful. Morality is absolute. Such color-blind moral thinking influences all ethical issues with which society is struggling, including stem-cell research, birth control, abortion, gay marriage, doctor-assisted suicide, war, state-church separation, teaching evolution, protecting the environment, animal rights, and global climate change. A religiously polarized brain cannot see that an ethical decision is often a compromise, a lesser of two evils, a contextual assessment of the relative merits of consequences, a practical matter. Fundamentalist believers require that there always be "One Right Answer," a code of Absolute Morality, when most of our lives are lived in the gray area—or the spectrum—of situational ethics. Sometimes there is no "right answer," as I showed in chapter 2 where reason and instinct sometimes conflict. As a result of polarized thinking, fundamentalists will often make horribly blunt ethical decisions. Holy war, opposition to birth control, killing abortion doctors, denying medical treatment to one's children (because the bible says prayer will heal the sick), corporal punishment, death penalty, opposition to science education, refusal to divorce an abusive spouse, and destruction of the environment (because this world is merely a stepping stone to eternity) are some examples.

I think "religious morality" is an oxymoron. Morality is morality, and qualifying it with the word "religious" does not strengthen it. It weakens it. (The same is true with the phrase "alternative medicine." Medicine is medicine. Sometimes "alternative medicine" actually works, and when it does we call it "medicine.") As I mention in the previous chapter, "religious morality" reduces human behavior to a monochromatic one-size-fits-all orthodoxy that is actually more dangerous than the broader humanistic principle of reducing harm. I think religion actually compromises moral judgment.

During my debate with Dinesh D'Souza at the University of Wisconsin, I announced that I would prove to that audience that religion actually compromises moral judgment. First, I told them this story:

> Suppose I break into the home of a loving Christian family. This mother, father, and two children are faithful church attenders who read the bible and pray every day. They are generous, good people who help others and witness for their faith in Jesus. I tie them up and shoot the dog. I drown their cat in the bathtub. Then I set the house on fire and they all die. When the police ask me, "Why did you do it?" I reply: "No reason. The Devil made me do it."

I said to the audience, "Raise your hands if you think I am a moral monster." Every hand in that room of 1,500 people went up. Then I told them a morally equivalent story:

> In the biblical Book of Job we read about a good "blameless and upright" family man who was faithful in worship yet endured horrible torture at the hand of the God he loved. Satan, with God's explicit permission, caused a huge wind to blow down a wall and kill Job's ten children. All of his thousands of animals were killed. (The bible doesn't say if he had a dog or a cat.) In Job 2:3 we find these words: "The LORD said to Satan, 'Have you considered my servant Job? There is no one like him on the earth, a blameless and upright

man who fears God and turns away from evil. He still persists in his integrity, although you incited me against him, to destroy him for no reason.'" So the police ask God, "Why did you do it," and God replies: "No reason. The Devil made me do it."

Then I said to the audience, "Raise your hands if you think the God of the bible is a moral monster." Less than half the hands shot up.

That is proof that hundreds of people in that room had eyes to see, but saw not. The same crime by two different actors for the same reason is judged morally wrong when committed by only one of the actors. This is a psychological bias induced by religion. It is "looking the other way," deliberately excusing the actions of a family member or other person you admire or love. It is what allows ministers and priests to get away with abusing children right under the noses of their parishioners who can't imagine their beloved leader would do anything wrong—or if it looks wrong, there must be a good reason for it. If your hand raised for both situations, you are able to make objective moral judgments. If you did not raise your hand for the second example, you are religiously colorblind and morally compromised.

Think about truth. Most fundamentalists demand that truth claims be absolute. In true polarized fashion, Jesus reportedly said, "All you need to say is simply 'Yes' or 'No'; anything beyond this comes from the evil one." Christians are required to think that any answer between the extremes comes from Satan! This might look like a simplistic or stubborn attitude, but it is much more dangerous. That polarized mind-set has got people killed.

John Calvin actually had his co-reformer Michael Servetus executed because he dared to challenge his absolute interpretation of the bible. Both men were opponents of the autocracy and legalism of Roman Catholicism and broke away from that "one true church." Protestants were protesters, after all. You might think this rebellious attitude would liberalize their thinking, and for some Protestants it did. But while Servetus continued to move in a flexible direction, free to think and question, Calvin made one hop away from Catholicism and then locked himself in place again. After Calvin wrote his *Institutes of the Christian Religion*, his Protestant theology became engraved in stone, turning into the new "one true faith." He could hardly admit error after that, so when good-hearted, trusting Servetus pointed out that Calvin had made a mistake about the biblical doctrine of the Trinity, he found himself arrested, wrongly convicted of blasphemy and heresy, and burned at the stake while Calvin watched. The killers used green wood for the fire so that his death would be prolonged, his own "heretical" book lashed to his body to go up in flames with him.

Servetus was murdered because of the misplacement of a preposition. His view of the nature of God was a different hue from Calvin's. Servetus had discovered that the New Testament does not actually teach the concept of the Trinity. (Hence, the birth of modern Unitarianism where the deity is not "God in three persons" but simply "one God.") There is only one verse in the bible that explicitly mentions the triune nature of God in three persons: "For there are three that bear record in heaven, the Father, the Word, and the Holy Ghost: and these three are one" (1 John 5:7). This is known as the Johannine Comma, because, as Servetus learned, it did not appear in any preceding Greek manuscripts of the biblical text. That verse had been interpolated into the more recent Latin Vulgate translation by the Catholic Church. Servetus eagerly brought this textual and doctrinal error to Calvin's attention, naively imagining he would welcome another opportunity to correct the fallacies of Catholicism. However, while rejecting Catholic orthodoxy, Calvin could not abandon the doctrine of a triune God. Since the Trinity was affirmed in Calvin's *Institutes,* and since truth is absolute, Servetus' "freethinking" attitude was deemed blasphemous (not to mention that his friend was challenging his authority and credibility).

Servetus had gone too far: he was proposing the heretical idea that opinions should be based on facts.

The main issue was the nature of Jesus. In trinitarian thinking, Jesus and the Holy Spirit are God, and have always been God. In unitarian thinking, Jesus only came into existence when he was born a human, when "the word became flesh." To unitarians, Jesus was just a man, the "son of God" (also called "the son of man") while he lived on earth. Servetus called him "Jesus, the son of the eternal God." Calvin called him "Jesus, the eternal son of God." See the difference? Does the rearrangement of a preposition and adjective merit the death penalty?

Calvin could have stopped the execution at any moment, and most historians think he would have done so if Servetus had recanted and apologized for his "error." But in the final moments of his agony, Servetus bravely called out, "Jesus, son of the eternal God, have mercy on me!" Hearing those words, Calvin, watching from a second floor, shut the window and let him die.[4]

John Calvin suffered from religious color blindness. (Not to mention arrogance, hatred, and malice.) There was only one way to look at the world. His way. He could not see that Servetus was indeed a friend—a smart friend with his own interpretation, a different frequency within the spectrum of Protestantism. In Calvin's mind, there was no prism, no latitude, no shades of gray, no hues of color. The Puritans of the Massachusetts Bay Colony brought Calvin's monochromatic rigidness with them to the American continent, and the United States is still dealing with that calcified mind-set to this day.

Fundamentalists have a desperate need to agree with each other 100 percent. To feel confident and unthreatened, the religiously color-blind need to know that all the members of their group are seeing the same color. "I appeal to you, brothers and sisters," Paul wrote, "in the name of our Lord Jesus Christ, that all of you agree with one another in what you say and that there be no divisions among you, but that you be perfectly united in mind and thought" (1 Corinthians 1:10).

He didn't explain how to choose the person who makes the decision that everyone else should agree with. He only suggested that those who don't go along with the crowd, those who think for themselves, should be kicked out of the group. "If your thoughts are not my thoughts, they are goodbye thoughts."

Fundamentalists need truth to be absolute. They are extremely uncomfortable with uncertainty or estimates of truth. They think truth is an object. Jesus said, "I am the truth." But a person cannot be the truth. Truth is not a thing. Truth is simply a measure of how well a statement matches reality. The only thing that can be true or false is a statement, a proposition. Reality is not truth: reality is reality. If the sky is blue and I say, "The sky is blue," then there is a strong correspondence between my statement and reality, so my statement would be true. If I say, "The sky is orange with black polka dots," there is a very low correspondence, so my statement would be false. Of course, the sky is always changing color (it is sometimes orange), and is dark during the night, so "the sky is blue" is a true statement that has to be qualified. It is not absolute.

In science and history, truth is always a matter of probability, not 100 percent certainty. Scientists talk about needing 95 percent confidence, or 98 percent confidence before claiming something is a fact, and even then it is qualified with a small amount of uncertainty. History is the weakest of the sciences, so weak that some do not consider it a science at all. Historians use words like "very unlikely," or "almost certainly," or "probably not," or "if the records are to be trusted," or "nearly universally rejected by scholars." Did Homer exist as an actual historical person? Maybe yes, maybe no. *The Iliad* and *The Odyssey* exist, so it is conceivable there was one person, possibly named Homer, who could not see blue, who wrote them. But some scholars think the poetry as we know it was a later compilation from earlier oral sources, edited, redacted, interpolated, and that even the earlier sources may have been compilations of poems from one or more persons. If by Homer we mean "a person or persons who wrote those earliest poems," then yes, Homer existed. But if we mean a specific person in history whose name was Homer who wrote the epics as we know them, then we have to back off and say "probably," or "probably not," depending on which scholarship we consult. However, if historians were fundamentalists, they would have to say "definitely yes" or "absolutely not," disallowing uncertainty. Fortunately, most historians are not colorblind.

The same is true with the existence of the historical Jesus. As I write in *Godless*, I think the probability of the existence of a historical person named Jesus, the founder of Christianity, is very low. I don't think it is zero, but I definitely think it is below 50 percent—maybe I would put it around 20 percent or 30 percent. Although I might be wrong, I am comfortable calling Jesus a myth. Bart Ehrman disagrees.[5] Ehrman is also a former preacher, like me, now a nonbeliever, and a biblical scholar who wrote *Did Jesus Exist?: The Historical Argument for Jesus of Nazareth*. He thinks it is higher than 50 percent, but even he admits it is not absolutely certain. I don't know what probability Bart would pick, but suppose I think it is 42 percent and he thinks it is 58 percent. Those two positions are not so far apart, but if we were forced to bluntly round it up or down, like a fundamentalist, then I would have to say "no" and he would have to say "yes." However, we don't *have* to round it off. We can accept the uncertainty, and remain flexible as we learn more. We can argue for our respective positions. In the future, I might raise my assessment or Bart might lower his. Of course, neither of us thinks in actual numbers, like a statistician, but that is possible to do. Some historians are using Bayes's Theorem to calculate more focused probabilities.[6]

Just to be clear, neither Ehrman nor I think Jesus as portrayed in the New Testament actually existed. There is a difference between the historical Jesus and the literary Jesus.[7] Perhaps there was a historical self-proclaimed messiah named Yeshua the Christ after whom the Gospels were based (there were others, such as Judas the Christ and

Theudas the Christ), but the supernatural miracle-working cartoon character precisely depicted in the Gospels did not exist. In that case, the New Testament is a kind of historical fiction. Since fundamentalist Christians claim to worship the Jesus of the New Testament, dismissing the existence of the literary Christ is the same as doubting that their Lord and Savior ever lived at all. Unable to think in shades of color, some of them claim I am a fundamentalist atheist who is saying Jesus never existed. I am not saying that at all. They fail to perceive the color difference between the historical Jesus and the New Testament Jesus. All I am saying is that the probability of the historical Jesus is very low (so I am open to adjusting my assessment), but the probability of the New Testament Jesus is so extremely low that we can safely round it down to zero, at least in informal conversation. If you don't understand the distinction, or the process, then you are religiously colorblind.

Paul Bunyan might be a useful comparison. It is possible that there indeed existed a large Canadian lumberjack named Paul Bunyan who fought with the French against the British in the early nineteenth century. We don't know, but we can't rule it out. We have a story, after all. However, the story was written down much later than the actual events. We also notice that the legend of a towering logger who dug the Great Lakes as a watering hole for his gigantic blue ox looks very much like a fable. The exaggerated fable might have been based on actual core events, but I think you would agree that the probability of the existence of the literary Paul Bunyan character (as portrayed in the story) is very close to zero, and that the probability of the existence of the historical Paul Bunyan is higher, perhaps 15 percent or 30 percent. In neither case do we have absolute certainty. It is possible that the entire tale is a myth. If you can live with that, then you can handle uncertainty. If you can't live with that same process of comparing probabilities between the core historical Jesus and the later story of the wonder-working New

Testament Jesus, then you are religiously colorblind. You have magically turned faith into fact, water into wine.

Truth is rarely black and white. (I wanted to write "never black and white," but that statement would be absolute. I need to allow that I might be wrong.) Forcing truth to be absolute is like making the rainbow a solid color, which is no rainbow at all.

The next time you talk with a true believer, remember that fundamentalists are religiously colorblind. That's what it *means* to be a fundamentalist. That includes the founder of Christianity. Jesus, if he existed, called himself "the Truth," and said, "He that is not with me is against me." He didn't understand neutrality. If you are not with him, that does not mean you are against him. You might not have enough information to decide one way or the other, waiting to make up your mind. You might prefer to think for yourself, not bringing "every thought into captivity," considering some of his teachings to be good, and others bad. You might see him in context, a product of an earlier era of magical thinking when gods and saviors popped up like dandelions, an honest (or not) preacher with a messiah complex and a handful of sometimes-useful platitudes. You might disagree with him entirely but grant him and his followers the freedom to believe as they choose. That doesn't mean you are "against him." You might admire much of his teachings but think perhaps some (or most) of those words were put into his mouth by the writers. But Jesus himself, if he existed and really said what the text reports, didn't grasp probability, subtlety, or tolerance. He and his orthodox followers are unable to see blue, like the ancient Greeks, or puce, like the modern author of this book. Understand them, don't bully them; they are differently abled.

When you are conversing with a fundamentalist, it might seem like you are both talking a foreign language. You might say "tolerance for all lifestyles," but they will hear "evil!" You may ponder the probabilities of the historicity of Jesus, but they will hear "Christ denier!" You might try to show that morality is situational and relative, and they will shout "reprobate!" You might affirm the right of women to control their reproductive future, and they will scream "baby killer!" They are the ones with the perceptual problem, not you.

Finally, think about purpose. To claim there is "a purpose of life" is to pound it flat. It's like saying all songs must be played in one key, all art painted in one color, and all sculptures carved from the same stone. That is true nihilism. There are many purposes in life, which makes life interesting, beautiful, challenging, sometimes fun, sometimes heartbreaking. To believe there is just one "purpose of life" is to deny the joyful dimensions of our existence. It turns us into robots. To live as a slave is dreary and depressing; to live free is bright and exciting. Both have their challenges, but only freedom gives you the chance to truly live and grow, to taste the varieties of experience, to hear the rich harmonies and see all the colors of the rainbow.

4

MUCH ADO ABOUT

I had a feeling once about Mathematics, that I saw it all—
Depth beyond depth was revealed to me—the Byss and the
Abyss. I saw, as one might see the transit of Venus—or
even the Lord Mayor's Show, a quantity passing through
infinity and changing its sign from plus to minus. I saw
exactly how it happened and why the tergiversation
was inevitable: and how the one step involved all
the others. . . . But it was after dinner and I let it go!
—Winston Churchill[1]

Why are we here?

I don't mean, "What is the meaning of it all?" I mean, "Why is there something rather than nothing?" Nothing comes from nothing, we often hear, so how can something come from nothing?

Those seem like great questions, and believers say the answer is God. Some nonbelievers are at a loss to reply: "The reason there is something rather than nothing is . . . just because." A witty response to "why is there something rather than nothing?" is "why not?" But that doesn't really answer the question.

"How can something come from nothing?" does sound provocative, but is it a valid question? Maybe "why is there something rather than nothing?" falls into that group of questions that look profound from the outside but when logically unpacked reveal hidden assumptions leading to circular logic or incoherence—what Daniel Dennett might call a Deepity Question. "What is south of the South Pole?" is such a question. If a minister were to ask in solemn tones from the pulpit, "Why is up not down?" some in the pews might wonder, "I never thought of that! Why *is* up not down?"

"Why *is* there something rather than nothing? How *can* something come from nothing?"

Before I try to unpack those questions, let's assume for a moment they are valid and look at the common response: "The reason there is something rather than nothing is because God created something out of nothing." That sounds straightforward, but is it an honest answer to an honest question? I think saying "God did it" is not really an answer: it is the reason for the question in the first place. Very few people initially come to their belief in a god by pondering metaphysical riddles. (Bertrand Russell did briefly, as a young man, but he very quickly jettisoned ontological arguments when he realized that they just boil down to "bad grammar.") "Why is there something rather than nothing?" is a question most nonphilosophers pose *after* they choose to believe in a supernatural world, in order to defend their faith. It is like asking, "If there is no god, who pops up the next Kleenex?" The question is shaped to lead to the answer they want. "Who caused the thunder?" the pagans asked. "Thor did!" Any question that starts with "who" assumes that the answer must be a person. This is known as begging the question.[2]

And if a nonbeliever replies honestly, "I don't know why there is something rather than nothing," believers will crow: "Aha! You don't have an answer, and I do!" This is known as a "god of the gaps" argument, or an argument from ignorance. Any mystery can be "solved" without doing any work, simply by plugging the hole with magic.

But let's be charitable and fair. On its face, the question is not necessarily religious. The motives of those who ask, "Why is there something rather than nothing?" may be honest and sincere, and even if not, that alone is no reason to dismiss their conclusion. Since something cannot come from nothing, their argument goes, and since something obviously exists, then it had to come from something else, and that something else could be (must be) "God!"

The obvious flaw with this reasoning is that a god is not nothing. A god is something. If something cannot come from nothing, then neither can a god. A god can also ask: "Why am I here? Why is there something rather than nothing? Why is there a god instead of no god?" If it is true that nothing comes from nothing, then God does not exist.

If you replace one mystery with another mystery, you still have a mystery.

What Is Nothing?

> *I got plenty o' nothin'*
> *And nothin's plenty for me.*
> —*Ira Gershwin*[3]

> *Nothing is real.*
> —*John Lennon*[4]

When asking "why is there something rather than nothing?," what does "nothing" mean? In English, it is a word broken into two parts: no + thing. The word "nothing" actually contains something: something to be negated. Linguistically, nothing is the absence of something. When we say there is nothing in a hole in the ground, we mean there is no dirt there. A hole is not a thing in itself: it is the lack of whatever is around that space. It depends on what the hole is surrounded by in order to know what is not there. A hole in the wall and a hole in the ice are not the same thing, but they are both holes, both nothing. What exactly is a doughnut hole? Or a cave? "What happens to the hole when the cheese is gone?" asked Bertolt Brecht.[5] If I see a pothole in the road, I know it is empty because I expect there to be a smooth, unbroken surface there. The pothole is not really empty—it is filled with air, or maybe water—but we still say there is nothing there. It is the absence of road that makes the pothole what it is.

Picture the pothole in the highway. Now take away the road around it. Erode the landscape down a few meters so that the space that used to be the pothole is now surrounded by nothing but air. Is the pothole still there? We don't define "nothing" by itself. We define it by the "thing" it is expected to be but is not. We define nothing by something. (It is the same in Latin. The phrase *ex nihilo* means "out of nothing." *Nihil* is from *ne* + *hilum,* which means "no + little thing." The word "nil" is a contraction of *nihil.*)

In other words, you can't have nothing without something. "Nothing" is not a thing. The question "can something come from nothing?" treats "nothing" as if it were a thing from which another thing could theoretically come (else why ask the question?), but that is backward. It is nothing that "comes from" something, not the other way around. It is like asking if a road can come from a pothole.

Looking at it that way, "can something come from nothing?" actually has a good answer. If you *have* the holes—if you are examining those "nothings"—then in a surprising way we can actually say that something indeed comes from nothing. If you have a pothole, you have a road. If I see a doughnut hole, I see a doughnut. If we have no money in the bank, we have a bank. If we have nothing, we have something.

In music, a rest is a symbol indicating that nothing is to be played for a certain length of time. It is a pause between notes. If you were to quickly enter the concert hall during a rest and exit before the end of it, you would have heard nothing: you could have said the musicians were not performing. But they *were* performing, and that rest is deliberate. The "hole" in the music gives emphasis to what preceded it and causes the listeners to anticipate what follows. The musicians are actually "playing nothing," which means something else exists around that space, before and after those notes. Miles Davis said, "Don't play what's there. Play what's not there." When I am improvising in a jazz combo, I often like to tease the listeners (and the other musicians) by *not* playing what they expect, such as the very last note of a dramatic phrase. Of course, the rhythm section is keeping time, but that's why it works. The listeners are waiting, so in that context, the nothing becomes something, like a doughnut hole. Jack Kerouac said, "It is only through form that we can realize emptiness." When a standup comic pauses before the punch line, does the crowd think nothing is happening? The musical rest and the pregnant pause are quite meaningful. "Art adores a vacuum," art critic Roberta Smith said. Those gorgeous "nothings" exist by virtue of what they are surrounded by.

If there is nothing, then there has to be something.

So, "can something come from nothing?" really means "can something come from something?" and that is a no-brainer. "Can something be what makes it different from what it is not?"

"Nothing" is just a word we use to identify absence. It is a concept, not a thing. The concept of absence can apply to things that are real as well as to things that are imaginary. The absence of Neanderthals and the absence of leprechauns are not measured the same way, but they end up the same. Absence is absence.

Since "nothing" is a concept, and concepts are a result, not a cause, of a brain, asking if something can come from nothing is like asking if a brain can come from a thought it is thinking.

What Is Nothingness?

In the quantum realm, even nothing never sleeps.
Nothing is always up to something.
—K. C. Cole[6]

The vacuum might even be the "source" of all matter in
the universe.
—Lawrence M. Krauss[7]

Some believers will agree this far but complain that I am equivocating. We are not dealing with potholes or bank accounts, they say. We are not talking about "nothing" in any particular example. The question "can something come from nothing?" really means "can something come from nothing-*ness*?" They are imagining an absolute void, a state of existence in which there actually are no things, no "something" anywhere that might give "nothing" its meaning.

But if nothingness is what is actually meant in the question, "can something come from nothing?" the problem does not go away. If nothingness is a state of existence, then it is something. A state of existence is not nothing. If you have a state, you have something that can be in a state. "The only way one can speak of nothing is to speak of it as though it were something," wrote Samuel Beckett.[8]

It does no good to counter that we are only talking about existence as a concept because if somethingness and nothingness are possible states of existence, then we are talking about a real thing: a reality that accommodates matter and energy even if it isn't there. I don't think existence is a thing (see below), but if believers want to talk about a state of existence, then they are saying it is a thing. Anything that can be in one of a plural number of states will have a certain potential for each of those possibilities. Therefore, in order for nothingness to truly be an optional state of existence, there must be a potential for another state to take its place. And how do we measure the likelihood of a potential state? The only way to get a probability is to divide one number by another. If nothingness and somethingness are two potential states of existence, we could estimate their probabilities by asking how many ways it is possible for nothing versus something to exist. There would be only one way for nothing to exist, but there is a very large number of ways for something to exist. By that logic, it is much more likely that something exists rather than nothing. Let's say there are a billion ways for something to exist. Assuming these all have equal weights, that would put the likelihood of nothingness at one in a billion plus one, or a 0.00000001 probability. Would you bet on that? Of course, it's much smaller than one in a billion. Nothingness is extremely unlikely. If the number of potential "somethings" is infinite, then something *must* exist.

Even if you think the odds are equal—that there is only one way for somethingness to be a state of existence, or that the number of nothingnesses is the same as the number of somethingnesses—then it is 50-50, with no preference for nothingness. But is that right? That would be like saying H_2O has a 50 percent chance of being ice or water, a grossly simplistic assumption (besides ignoring the possibility of a gas). Strangely, even if the odds were truly 50-50, many believers would still feel that nothingness is more likely than somethingness. If reality is the result of a coin flip, heads needs an explanation while tails does not? If there were nothing at all, these same people would probably protest: "Why is there nothing rather than something?!" They might imagine a supernatural being using its power to restrain somethingness from invading the void. But where do we get the idea that nothing is stronger than something? Why do we assume that reality, unmanaged, collapses to nothingness? Is it like gravity? The path of least resistance? From whence comes the great power of the void? (And if the void has this power, then it has something.) Perhaps it is the other way around: the great power of matter and energy is holding back the void. "Nature abhors a vacuum," Aristotle thought.

But that all seems pretty silly, because something/nothing is not a proper yin/yang. They are not balanced opposites of a composite whole. If they were, then zero would be the reciprocal for every other number and math would be meaningless. But one thing we do know—and if there were a god, he/she would know it too—is that something indeed does exist, so there is no argument. Reality has not decayed into nothingness, or remained in such a state, not in the natural world or the supernatural world (if there is such a place). In fact, if there were truly nothingness, there would be no reality at all, natural or supernatural. We are aware of the reality that something does exist. That's what reality means. Whatever the Theory of Everything (TOE) turns out to be, there will come a point where we simply have to refer to a brute fact—perhaps strings or branes or quantum wave potential, or something else. That is exactly what theists do when they refer to their brute fact of an intricate creator mind with desires and elaborate rules magnificently orchestrating the natural world from a supernatural platform, sticking his TOE into our world, though I don't see how an absurdly complicated brute fact should be more likely than the simpler brute facts uncovered by science.

But let's give the believers a chance to define their terms. If the phrase "nothing comes from nothing" makes sense, we need to know what those words mean. Close your eyes and try to picture complete nothingness. What do you see? Perhaps you see darkness, emptiness, absolute coldness, zero Kelvins, silence. But you see *something*. Aren't you picturing it in space and time? Aren't you imagining a vast open area that is devoid of all matter and light? If you are seeing "nothing there," you are at least picturing a "there" there. Or if you are like me, you are trying to conceive of an infinitely small dot—an iDot—devoid of all space, time, matter, energy, potential. But still, I am imagining that invisible, dimensionless weightless iDot hanging there, surrounded by all the potential everything that reality could actually be but isn't. And I can't help intuitively framing the iDot floating in space. The truth is that actual nothingness cannot be pictured or imagined in any way. Nothingness is something, isn't it? The only way to conceive of utter nothingness is not to conceive of anything at all. You have to be asleep, or in a coma, or dead, to do that. There is no way to know what nothing means. So the phrase "nothing comes from nothing(ness)" contains an incoherent or unintelligible word. Those who preach its possibility are mumbling iDots.

But let's try to keep going. Let's pretend we can indeed talk coherently about nothingness, just like we can talk about and even use imaginary numbers in equations without knowing how to picture them (if we can't imagine them, why are they called imaginary numbers?), or how we use zero as a placeholder. Not all words have objective or coherent referents, but perhaps "nothingness" might still be useful in spite of our lack of imagination.[9] Let's say that the "state of nothingness," at least, would be a complete absence of matter, energy, space, and time. But those are not the only things it would lack. It would also lack laws. The state of nothingness would lack a law that says "nothing comes from nothing." How's that for a brain twister? In a state of utter nothingness, with no restrictions (because there is nothing to restrict), everything is possible! Physics Nobel Laureate Frank Wilczek wrote: "The answer to the ancient question 'Why is there something rather than nothing?' would then be that 'nothing' is unstable."[10]

A believer might object that laws can only apply to actually existing things and that in a state of nothingness laws are meaningless because there would be nothing to apply them to. Besides the fact that this admits that nothingness is not an actually existing thing (so why talk about it?), remember that we are talking about a *state* of nothingness. Believers think that there is a state of reality that could be either nothing or something. If a state is one possible form of reality, then there must be something keeping it in that state, preventing it from entering a different form of reality, such as low temperature keeping ice from changing into water. But if utter nothingness were the state of reality, then there would exist no conditions, no barriers to prevent it from turning into another state. In such a lawless state, all things are possible, including one state becoming another, something coming from nothing. Spontaneously. All without a god.

And that is not so hard to imagine. Even in our own merely natural universe, it happens all the time. If by "nothing" we mean a completely empty vacuum devoid of all matter, then something indeed comes from nothing. Empty space contains seething quantum potential from which matter and energy emerge. In a tiny volume of a total vacuum, trillions of particles of matter and antimatter are randomly coming into existence out of nothing and then immediately annihilating each other, canceling each other out, the net effect of which is nothing. It is a weird invisible subatomic froth that produces utter silence. Physicist Lawrence M. Krauss describes it as "a boiling brew of virtual particles that pop in and out of existence in a time so short we cannot see them directly."[11] However, sometimes the two matter/antimatter particles become separated. For example, if they happen to come into existence at the exact event horizon of a black hole where only the antimatter particle falls in, then matter emerges from the void.[12] *Voilá*, something from nothing.

So in the real world, something *does* come from nothing.

This certainly sounds counterintuitive, but science is not guided by our intuitions. Science does not follow us; we follow the science. Krauss, in his book *A Universe From Nothing*, points this out nicely:

> [S]omething can arise from empty space *precisely* because the energetics of empty space, in the presence of gravity, are *not* what common sense would have guided us to suspect before we discovered the underlying laws of nature. . . . [N]o one ever said that the universe is guided by what we, in our petty myopic corners of space and time, might have originally thought was sensible. It certainly seems sensible to imagine that a priori, matter cannot spontaneously arise

from empty space, so that *something,* in this sense, cannot arise from *nothing.* But when we allow for the dynamics of gravity and quantum mechanics, we find that this commonsense notion is no longer true. This is the *beauty* of science, and it should not be threatening. Science simply forces us to revise what is sensible to accommodate the universe, rather than vice versa.[13]

Of course, a believer might object that since the vacuum contains quantum potential, it is not really empty. But we could say the same thing about the "state of nothingness" vacuum. Anything that has a state has a potential, quantum or otherwise. If reality has the potential to be either something or nothing, then like the vacuum of space, it is not empty either. If it has no potential, quantum or otherwise, it is no state at all. If nothingness has no potential, then nothing can't exist.

Theoretical physicist Stephen Hawking thinks our entire universe, not just particles, has arisen from the void. "Because there is a law such as gravity, the universe can and will create itself from nothing. Spontaneous creation is the reason there is something rather than nothing, why the universe exists, why we exist," Hawking writes. "It is not necessary to invoke God to light the blue touch paper and set the universe going."[14]

Nothing Is Perfect

> *The place of God in my soul is blank.*
> —*Mother Teresa*[15]

One way to show why Bertrand Russell thought the ontological argument was bad grammar is to point out its *reductio ad absurdum* when applied to something other than God. Anselm's eleventh-century version of the ontological argument went something like this:

1. God is a being than which no greater being can be conceived.

2. If God exists only in conception, and not in reality, then he could be conceived to be greater than he is.

3. Therefore, God must exist in reality.[16]

This silly argument was countered in Anselm's day by Gaunilo, who used it to "prove" the existence of a perfect island.[17] But we could do the same thing with nothingness:

1. Utter nothingness is a void than which no greater void can be conceived.

2. If utter nothingness exists only in conception, and not in reality, then it can be conceived to be greater than it is.

3. Therefore, utter nothingness must exist in reality.

Therefore, nothing exists. Putting the two bad-grammar arguments together, we could prove that God is Utter Nothingness.

What Is Something?

> What if everything is an illusion and nothing exists?
> In that case, I definitely overpaid for my carpet.
> —Woody Allen[18]

There is a deeper problem, one that is logically fatal. A slippery sleight-of-hand occurs when we change the question from "can something come from nothing?" to "can somethingness come from nothingness?" To treat those questions equally is to commit a category error. If you think they are equivalent, you will apply the assumptions from the first question to the second question, and a god or supernatural world will magically appear. (Now *that's* something from nothing!) But "something" and "somethingness" are not the same. "Something" refers to an object within the universe, but "somethingness" refers to the cosmos, the entire multiverse, all of reality.

If we are looking at "something," any particular thing in the universe, then indeed we can ask about its origin. Where did it come from? What is it made of? What properties does it have, and why? What color is it? How much does it weigh? How much space does it take up? Who or what forces made it? How was it assembled? Does it have a purpose? How old is it? How long will it exist? How does it relate to other things? We might even ask "why is it here?" but notice that that question, like all the others, implies that the object resides within a context larger than itself. You can't have a naked "why." To ask why is to reach out beyond the object to explain its cause, purpose, or origin by referring to something other and earlier, or contingently antecedent "out there." So to ask "why is there something rather than nothing?" is simply to assume there is a transcendent realm. Presto! God exists.

There are two good reasons we can't do that. The first is the category error. You can't take a finding from one logical level and apply it to a higher level. For example, every soldier is under the authority of a higher-ranking member of that army, but that fact applies only within the army, not to the army itself. We can't reason from that fact that every army on the planet is therefore under the authority of another army. Some armies are under no authority at all, most are under the authority of a government (a nonarmy), and although armies sometimes cooperate, it is certainly not true that the armies of the world are arranged in a hierarchical chain of command like the members within those armies. If so, there would be no need for armies! You can't treat "army" the same way you treat "member of the army." You can't treat molecules the same way you treat the atoms that make the molecules. In the same way, you can't treat "somethingness" (the group) the same way you treat "something" (an item in the group). You can't say that since "something" has to come from something else, then "something-ness" also has to come from something else. That is a category error, mixing logical spheres—which is a polite way to say it is illogical.[19]

The second reason we can't ask "why is there something(ness) rather than nothing(ness)?" is because "somethingness" is an incoherent term. Like "nothingness," we really don't know what it means. Is it the quality of being a material object? As opposed to what? Why do we pretend that by bootstrapping up from "something" to the higher logical sphere of "somethingness" we have done anything meaningful? "Somethingness" is not a thing or a quality of anything. If we say it is a "thing," then we are referring to some supposedly known context within which it resides, a context that is excluded from existence, which is like saying "existence doesn't exist" or "thingness is not a thing." Neither can "somethingness" be a quality or characteristic of existence. We can't say existence is blue, or heavy, or silent, or irritable. We can't say it has actuality, or "somethingness." At most "something-ness" would be a synonym for existence. (The same fallacy occurs in most forms of the ontological argument when a God who exists in actuality is compared with a God who exists only in conception, treating existence as if it were merely a property of an object.) "Something," any particular thing, might indeed exist or not, but "somethingness" is simply a label for "anything or everything that exists." Realizing this, the phrase "why is there something rather than nothing?" reduces to the incoherent "why does existence exist?" It's like the children who constantly ask "why?" after every answer, imagining they are doing something profound, confounding their parents. We could all play that game with logical spheres, composing syntactically correct but meaningless or ambiguous questions: "What is harmony in harmony with?" "How is digestion digested?" "What do thoughts think of?" "What is it that is conscious of consciousness, and what is conscious of *that*?" "How does conception conceive?" (Answer: immaculate conception.)

We can't ask, "Why does existence exist?" Existence does not have a context. Existence is not a thing. The verbs "to exist" and "to be" are just language. If there were no minds forming language, there would be no "existence," no question of whether something is or is not. Reality would just be reality. "To be" is a special kind of intransitive verb, treated differently in different languages. Although Russian does have a formal "to be," most people tend not to use it. For "you are my friend," they usually say "you my friend," and for "that is all," they say "that all." This is not because "to be" is implied, but because it is unnecessary. Spanish and Portuguese tease out the difference between where you are and what you are with two different verbs for "to be" (*estar* and *ser*), showing that "being" is syntactical, not a thing or a quality. I think "to exist" is just a way of putting words together, which is what "syntax" means. "Existence" is a label for a philosophical concept, not a name of anything out there. To "be a thing" is not to "have existence." The verb "to exist" represents the appearance of an object within a mind. There might be a rich vein of gold under the ground in my back yard, and there might not. But to say that there "is" or "is not" such a treasure is to say that "I know" something. That vein of gold might actually be there, but it is not saying, "Look at me! I'm existing!" (Should I go look for it?) It is only minds, which use language, that need to put it into words. If it is not there, it doesn't mean anything real to say "it has no existence," because "it" was nothing to begin with. It was just a concept. (Philosophers and scientists indeed talk about hypotheticals, but this is precisely because they are resisting the temptation to jump to conclusions.) Likewise, if it *is* there, saying "it is in existence" does not create the reality. It only creates the truth in the mind. Truth is just the degree with which a statement happens to correspond with reality. We only say "it exists" for our own sakes, to hold an image of reality in our brains. Bertrand Russell might have said that "why does something exist rather than nothing?" is another example of bad grammar.

Where Did It All Come From?

> *In the beginning there was nothing. God said, "Let there*
> *be light!" And there was light. There was still nothing,*
> *but you could see it a whole lot better."*
> —*Ellen DeGeneres*[20]

Notice that when we ask "can something come from nothing?" we are playing a loaded game similar to "who caused the thunder?" We are swallowing the claim that something, anything, always has to "come from" something or someone else. If we do that, we are forced to look for a "what" or a "who."

When we ask "can something come from nothing?" what do we mean by "come from"? I think there are two normal usages of that phrase: impersonal and personal. In ordinary usage, "comes from" means something physical and impersonal. A house "comes from" lumber or stone or building material. The lumber comes from trees, the stone from quarries, the bricks from mud, the nails and hardware from metal. A tree comes from a seed, the stone and metal comes from physical processes in the earth and the stars. And so on. These are all sufficient answers. So asking where the universe "came from" in that sense would be asking for the location of a huge quarry or forest of materials from which the construction materials were obtained, such as learning that the heavy elements that make up the earth were cooked up from hydrogen inside a star. That is not what believers mean when they ask that question. If we *were* to find a mammoth cosmic quarry from which the universe was chopped, we would simply ask where *that* came from.

The other usage is personal, dealing with minds rather than materials. We can say that a house "comes from" the mind of an architect, or from the skills of the carpenters and masons, and so on. In that sense, we are thinking "who?" rather than "what?" In the first usage, the suspects will be a line-up of physical things, but in the second usage, it will be a lineup of persons. And that is what turns the question into a circular argument, if "God" is the conclusion. If "comes from" means "be created by a person," then "can something come from nothing?" unpacks to "is it possible for something to be created by nobody?" or "can something come from no person?" *Voilá.* Who pops up the next Kleenex?

This whole question, then, boils down to believers challenging us skeptics to provide an impersonal answer to the origin of all of existence, and if we can't, they fold their arms and claim that the personal answer wins by default.

Does everything need a source? Why do we think that something always has to "come from" something else? And if it does, why doesn't God? Believers claim that our universe is contingent (how do they know that?), and the question "can something come from nothing?" applies only to things that have a source, a beginning, a cause, like our universe (how do they know that?), and that since God does not have a source (how do they know that?), there is no need to ask where he "came from."[21] But even if the universe did "come from" somewhere else, and even if we never find an impersonal answer (we haven't stopped searching), and even if there is a God (and that is a hugely unwarranted stretch of imagination), and even if his existence is necessary and not contingent, and even if God himself did not come from anywhere, and even if God has the power to create, it doesn't follow that God is the explanation of where the universe came from. If he exists, he might be the prime suspect—the best possible explanation, fitting the profile, lacking an alibi, even possessing a motive for the crime—but his guilt would have to be proved, not assumed. He is innocent until proven guilty. He might not want the blame. God and the cosmos might be siblings: they might exist side by side and our universe might have some other explanation, such as having "come from" a higher natural super-universe that was the cause of its own existence and even the cause of the existence of God. (Not supernatural, but "naturalsuper.") I have no reason to believe that contrived scenario, but it is no less fantastic than theism.

Where Did God Come From?

> *God is a spirit.*
> —*John 4:24*

There is no good reason to believe in a god, but if such a being exists, he also should ask himself, "Why am I here? Why is there a god instead of no god?" Most believers will claim that a god would never ask where it came from because a god is a great spirit outside of nature. The "great spirit" is above the law: you can't haul in the king for questioning, they insist. A spirit, they say, unlike us physical creatures, can indeed exist without an explanation, timeless, causeless, not needing a frame of reference or context. They imagine that there are actually three states of existence: nothing, something, and *spirit*. It is spirit that mediates between nothing and something, they claim. Spirit can cause something to come from nothing. God was looking around one day, saying, "There is nothing, and I don't like it, so I am going to turn nothing into something. *Fiat lux ex nihilo.* Lo, behold, now something exists!"

But does this make sense? Believers use the word "spirit" as if it were a substance or force that has the power to create matter,[22] or to manipulate matter, which means that "spirit" must have *some* material property in order to interface with natural objects. In order to have an effect, a spirit has to be *something*. If by something we mean not nothing, and by nothing we mean not something (the law of excluded middle), then there is no halfway house. A spirit, whatever it is, must be either something or nothing. If it is not something, it is nothing.

By the way, if God is defined as "a spirit," then spirit is something that God is made of. So spirit is not God. It is something more basic, otherwise God could not be "a spirit."

Some believers will reply that a spirit is indeed "something," but it is not "something natural." The question "can something come from nothing?" really means "can something *natural* come from nothing?" The supernatural or spiritual realm (which *they* have conjured out of nothing) is exempt from the question, they insist. Their three states of existence really are: nothing, *nature*, and spirit. We are natural creatures asking a natural question—a question about the entire notion and existence of "natural"—and the only sensible answer, they claim, must come from outside nature. Every question has a frame of reference, and the answer must come from within the frame, outside of the object in question. The explanation of one thing can't be the same as the thing itself, so the source of nature can't be nature. It has to be something else, other-natural, supernatural, spiritual, they insist. (Of course, these same people concede that the explanation of at least one thing—God—*can* be the same as the thing itself.)

But they are just chasing their tails. The argument begs the question, assuming the very thing it is trying to prove. When we use the terms as they define them, notice how the conclusion loops around and shows its face (or its tail), barely masked in the premises: "Nothing that is not supernatural can come from nothing. Something that is not supernatural exists. Therefore something that is not supernatural must have come from something else, and the only other place it could have come from is the supernatural. This proves that the supernatural exists!" Since the supernatural world is the very thing they are trying to prove, inserting that conclusion into their premises is circular logic. They should establish the existence of the supernatural world *before* they use it in an argument.

If it is true that nothing comes from nothing—that something cannot come from nothing, that something has to come from something—then a god, being something, had to come from something else. If a god came from nothing, then it can't be said that nothing comes from nothing. If a god did it, why can't a universe? They are both something.

If nothing comes from nothing, and if God came from nothing, then God is nothing.

Most believers insist that that is equivocating. We can't compare God and the universe like that. God is a special case: he is great and personal and powerful and, unlike the impersonal lifeless universe, he has the ability to create himself. But how does that help their argument? If they say that "nothing comes from nothing" really means "nothing except God-who-is-great comes from nothing," well there you go. They are back to question begging, inserting the conclusion into the premise. What could be a clearer example of circular logic? If you already believe in a god before you make the argument, then you don't need the argument at all. It should be discarded. If believers agree that *they* don't need the argument, but think that we atheists do—as a tool of evangelism—then they still need to convince us to embrace their "except God" qualification before we can get the argument off the ground, and if we did, we wouldn't need the argument because we would no longer be atheists. "Nothing comes from nothing" might be useful to theologians, philosophers, and songwriters, but it would no longer have value as an argument to convince those of us with a "wicked childhood" to change our minds and believe in God.

If a god can answer the question "why am I here?" with "just because," then so can we.

When I was a preacher I would have thought the previous sentence was utter foolishness, maybe even blasphemous. How can we compare ourselves with God? God is so much *bigger*, I believed. We are puny contingent beings. We are limited. We have good reason to ask "why am I here?" God does not. He is not dependent on anything. We are born and we die; God does neither. He is the Creator. He is all-powerful. The king does not ask "who is above me?" God is "I am that I am" who needs no explanation.

But when believers say God is "big" and "powerful," what do they mean? Those are words of dimension, force, and time. Can the word "big" mean something without measuring along dimensions? Can the word "power" be understood without plotting work across a span of time? If God is truly outside those dimensions, then what does it matter if he is called "big" and "powerful"? Those words have no meaning outside of the natural world, if it is possible to be "outside" of the natural world. Or if they *do* have a meaning outside the natural world, they have no meaning to *us*. We may as well say "God is bliphish and pomthical." God talk is nonsensical. He is the holy iDot.

If God is truly outside of somethingness, he is nothing at all.

What Is Spirit?

> *If you can see the invisible, God will do the impossible.*
> —Joel Osteen[23]

> *The invisible and the nonexistent look very much alike.*
> —Delos McKown[24]

But maybe we atheists are still missing something. Perhaps believers have tapped into a special reality, or have a different way of tapping into reality that I am unable to perceive. The spiritual world might indeed exist in spite of our lack of comprehension or imagination. If so, believers need to define their terms so that we blind skeptics can understand what those with superior vision are talking about.

When believers claim that a spirit caused something to come from nothing, what do they mean by "spirit"? What does "spirit exists" mean? Dealing with real entities, not abstract concepts, to exist means to occupy space and time. "To occupy" means that matter and/or energy takes up some amount of space and time, so if a spirit truly exists, it must be a substance or force in space and time.

In the Book of Acts, the early Christians were "filled with the spirit," which came to them as "tongues of fire."[25] I doubt that happened, but the storyteller or mythmaker is informing us that those proto-Christians were initially lacking something that then came to them from somewhere else. It "filled" them up. In this story, Jesus had promised his followers that "you will receive power when the Holy Spirit comes upon you," which means that they did not have this "spirit" until the Day of Pentecost when a tongue-shaped flame came zooming into them, causing them to speak in different languages. (Babbling iDots.) But notice that this surgical strike from outer space targeted only believers and left the bodies of non-Christians alone. There was no collateral damage. The bible certainly treats "spirit" as if it has locality, as something that occupies space and time, attaching itself to a body. If you can have it and I can't, then it is there and not here. Other religious traditions seem to hold a similar concept. Even those religions that claim spirit is everywhere and you have to tune into it, like a radio receiver, still mainly consider that each person perceives its own special portion of spirit. Most believers think that when they go to heaven their spirits will be distinct from each other, not just some huge amorphous blob of ether. Christians think they are going to meet Grandma in the afterlife. Here on earth, they say, a person's "spirit" follows their body around, and (usually) stays out of other bodies. So a spirit must be something—somewhere.

When we say that something exists, we mean it can be measured. It occupies so many units of the three dimensions during so many units of time. It can be staked out, clocked, and weighed. If it can't be measured, then we can't say it exists. We might say it exists as a concept, not in reality—like the average number of children—but that is equivocating, confusing two different usages of "exist." However, since a concept is a function of a physical brain, we *could* play a game and say that a "spirit exists" in the group of neurons that are temporarily firing while that concept is being represented. We could count the neurons involved and thereby weigh a "spirit," or rather the weight of the neurons used to form the concept of spirit. But all concepts would weigh virtually the same, just as the recipes for angel food cake and German chocolate cake (or anything else) weigh the same, or like photographs of a violet and a volcano weigh the same. This is not what believers mean when they say "spirit exists." Years ago the famous ether used to "exist" in many brains, but after Einstein, nobody thinks it is real. Notice that "spiritual" and "ethereal" are synonyms.

During my very first visit to Australia—in fact, my very first day, the morning after I arrived in Sydney in March 2010—I debated Cardinal George Pell at MacQuarie University on the topic of "Without God, We Are Nothing." Pell was the Archbishop of Sydney. Today he is Number 3 at the Vatican, as the prefect of the Secretariat for the Economy, Pope Francis's new finance ministry. If anyone is an expert in the faith, it would be "His Eminence Cardinal Pell." (I couldn't bring myself to use that title: he called me "Dan," so I called him "George.") During the debate, he used the word "spirit" and "spiritual" a number of times, so during cross examination, I asked him this question:

Dan: Can you define for us, using positive terms, what is a "spirit," and how that would differ from nothing at all?

George: I just said that I can't define "God," but I can say something useful about "spirit." I believe in the reality of love. I believe it's a spiritual quality. I believe honor is something that is real. Disgrace is real. Forgiveness is real. Something spiritual is invisible, but sometimes it can be very powerful. The love of a husband and wife, the love between parents and children, they are probably the most important realities in many people's lives. They are spiritual realities.

Dan: Let me follow up. I can define all of those things, like love, family, and feelings, in purely natural terms, as functions of an organism. But why were you not begging the question by saying that the definition of "spiritual" is love, which is spiritual? I want to know what it *is*. Does it occupy space? Does it occupy time? Does it have a weight? Can you measure it along a dimension? How would you know that your "spirit" is not just a concept as opposed to an actually existing thing in reality?

George: Well, you can't measure a spirit. It is certainly not material. But the examples that I have given are very real and very powerful. Once there was an Australian poet who said that sometimes people can be at a concert and be like dogs at a concert. They hear every sound but have got no understanding of the music, because the music is something that is spiritual and beautiful and real. They can't be reduced. They are connected with physical activities, but they can't be reduced to those physical activities.

So I'm a dog, but I take that as a compliment. Notice that Pell said "spirit" is immaterial and invisible and can't be measured, but it has *power*. Does he not know that power is measured materially? He sidestepped telling us what a "spirit" actually *is*. When believers are asked to define what "spirit" actually *is*—not to list synonyms like ghost, vision, or poltergeist; or attitudes like enthusiasm, love, emotion, or determination; but to describe the actual substance of the entity—they always define it by what it is not: intangible, noncorporeal, immaterial, ineffable, non-natural. (They might even say "the spirit is the ethereal essence.") They never tell us anything positive. How big is it? How much does it weigh? What is its surface and how does it stay within those boundaries? What is its opacity? If they can't give us a measurable definition, then they are giving us nothing but a couple of syllables of sound. They tell us that this . . . thing . . . blah blah . . . ether . . . this word without a definition exists outside of space and time, and is in fact the very . . . *thing* . . . blah blah . . . that possesses power to create something from nothing. They tell us that supernatural entities cannot be described in natural terms. Even though the rest of us can't coherently hold the word in our heads, somehow they know that "it" exists.

When I say that something that cannot be measured cannot exist, they respond that there is another way something can exist: outside of space and time.

So who is equivocating? To say that something cannot come from nothing unless spirit makes it happen is to say nothing at all. "Something" is a measurable entity; "spirit" is not. To say that "existence as we understand it exists as we don't" is incoherent.

Here is a little poem I wrote for Steven Pinker, after hearing one of his talks, that I might set to music:

F-WORDS
Mystery and Ecstasy and other treble-clef words
Hint that what is Spiritual is truly inexpressible,
But the fact that Fable, Faith, and Fantasy are F-words
Shows that what is Mystical is not at all ineffable.

What Is Outside?

Pay no attention to that man behind the curtain.
—*The Wizard of Oz*

Even if spirit does exist in some unknowable way—in spite of my impertinence in asking for a definition—what do believers mean when they say it is "outside" of nature? Exactly where is that? If a spirit is outside of nature, it still must be somewhere, in a region "beyond." And that is still a place. Something might indeed be outside our own observable universe in the wider cosmos, but how can anything be outside of nature? Universes within the multiverse would certainly be outside of each other, but they would still be part of the natural cosmos. If we don't have a coherent definition of "outside of nature," then it is meaningless to suggest that that is *where* the spirit or supernatural *exists*.

Some think that to be outside of nature is to be in another dimension. But that is incoherent. Dimensions are used to measure natural things. Dimensions are what we *mean* when we say something is natural: the object occupies space and time, which are charted in four dimensions, at least. The amounts of space and time that an object occupies are measured along those dimensions compared to other objects, or the distance between other objects, which give us units of measurement. If there are more than four dimensions, and there indeed may be (especially if some form of string theory or M-theory is correct), then what is measured along those additional dimensions would also be natural. Dimensions are not things. Dimensions are not places or regions or realms we can visit. Dimensions are not outside or inside of each other: they are frames of reference that give the words "there," "region," "outside," and "before" the meanings that they have. They are conceptual and mathematical frames of reference that we use to measure whether one thing is inside or outside of another. If you are currently outside of my house, you are still in four dimensions (at least). Since "outside" is determined by locating an object at dimensional coordinates not contained by the space/time occupied by another object, the word cannot apply to anything other than nature itself, by definition. To say a spirit is "outside of nature" is to say it is "outside of outside," treating a dimension itself as if it were a thing being measured along that dimension.

It makes no sense to talk of measuring a dimension. "How high is height?" and "how wide is width?" are incoherent questions. No matter what units you use, the answer is always infinite, which is no answer at all.

Time is a dimension. To say that God is outside of time is to say "God is never." Until believers clarify their words, it is meaningless to say that a spirit is outside of nature. "Somewhere, over the rainbow" is still somewhere.[26]

What Is Possible?

Dividing by zero is the closest thing there is to arithmetic blasphemy.
—William Dunham[27]

"Can something come from nothing?" might be unanswerable because it is unaskable. Logically, mathematically unaskable.

Think of it as division. The basic idea of "come from," as we saw, breaks an object down into smaller parts. A house "comes from" lumber, bricks, mortar, nails—trees, clay, iron—and so on. It can be divided into smaller units that add up, or multiply (because multiplication is merely successive addition) to a final product. A house (h) made of 4,000 bricks (b) could be shown as "h=4,000b" or "b=h/4,000." Almost everything can be said to be composed of (divided by) atoms that originated somewhere else. A simple rock is made of elements that were cooked up inside a star, and those elements migrated by gravity from somewhere else. An airplane and an asteroid are made of (divided by) the elements that multiply (add) to make the final product. We could break it down further into subatomic particles, but we are still breaking it down. Even in cases where it looks like something came from something larger than itself, such as a statue carved out of a chunk of marble or a thermos filled with water from a lake, those larger sources are themselves composed of the same smaller elements.

Someday, if we do find something that is not broken down into other parts—the Prime Particle, let's say—we will say that it is divided by itself, and stop there. (That's what the word "atom" means: "not cut or divided," though we quickly learned that we applied the term prematurely to a group of what we now have to call "subatomic particles," so an atom is not really an "atom" at all.) Someone might wonder if that Prime Particle could be further subdivided, but that would increase the denominator, not decrease it. It would never be less than one. (Dividing by less than one makes a number larger, not smaller.) We would never ask of anything, "Can it be broken down into zero parts?" By definition, the number of parts of an object must be greater than zero, and greater than one. If it is one, then it has no parts.

Division by zero is one of those mathematical impossibilities that lead equations to absurdities and cause computers to crash. On its face, asking if twelve can be divided by zero looks like an honest question: "What is 12/0?" But logically, mathematically, it is incoherent. Such a question is not just illegal: it is not allowed because it is not possible. It has no comprehensible answer. This is easy to prove. When you divide one number by another you can check your result by multiplying it by the original divisor. To prove that 12/4=3, you simply multiply 3x4=12. That is logical because division is just reverse multiplication, which is addition. It is really no different from saying that 12-4=8 can be confirmed by 8+4=12. But how would you confirm the answer to 12/0? If you think 12/0=0, then check it out: you get 0x0=0, not 0x0=12. There is no way to get back to your original number. If you think the answer is one, then 12/0 is equal to 12/12, which is illogical, and still checks out to zero when you multiply. If you think the answer is infinity, you still don't get back to 12 because infinity times zero is zero. The only way to get a number back to itself is to divide by one: 12/1=12, which checks to 12x1=12. That's just another way of saying something is what it is.

Computer programmers know that a system will crash if an attempt is made to divide by zero, so a specific check for that danger has to be hard-coded into the software. When computers are asked to divide by zero, the calculation is not made; it is sidestepped. No answer is given. No answer is possible. Some systems handle it gracefully with an alert, and others simply stop. (Try it on your calculator to see what happens.) If the programmers don't guard against it, the system will go crazy. Notice that the result of trying to divide by zero is not "nothing."

That would be saying it is zero. The result is no answer at all. It is utter meaninglessness.

Now follow this: asking if something can come from nothing is just like asking if it can be divided by zero. You can't say yes, no, or maybe. "What is s/0?" Don't even try to reply. It is not a valid question.

The reason we cannot divide by zero—the reason it is a nonsensical question—is because "divide" means to "share." It's where we get the phrase "divvy up." How can three children share twelve cookies? By giving four cookies to each child. But if you don't have any children who want the cookies, then it makes no sense to talk about sharing the cookies. You can only share (divide) when you have a positive nonzero number of divisors (children). If the number of numerators (cookies) is negative, we are talking about sharing a debt, which is the same thing in obverse. If the number is zero, we can't talk about sharing at all. We wouldn't ask, "How can no children share twelve cookies?" They can't because they don't exist. Division becomes meaningless. Although dividing (sharing) and "coming from" are not identically parallel concepts, they both require a nonzero divisor. A computer function called "Share()," for example, might accept any numerical parameter, including zero, but inside the function it better trap the zero or it will crash. Most programmers know that it is better to trap the mistake before it even gets into the function. Don't even go there. Sharing doesn't work with zero. You wouldn't say "the cookies are shared by zero children," you would say "the cookies are not shared at all." In the same way, we would not say "something comes from nothing," we would say "something does not come from anything at all." It completely turns things upside down when we change "not come from anything" to "come from nothing." It turns nothing into something, which is why you can't divide by zero. When we say "something comes from nothing," we mean it doesn't come from anything, not that it actually comes from nothing. It doesn't have to come from anything. It divides by one. It simply exists on its own.

Some believers might think this actually makes their case because it proves that something cannot have come from nothing, but that is the point. It "comes from nothing" not in the sense that "nothing" is its source, but in the sense that it doesn't come from anything at all, in the same sense that the cookies are not shared by zero children, but are not shared at all. It's not that something can or cannot come from nothing; it's that the question is bogus. A nonsensical question can't be the basis for any conclusion. It is true that we can't divide by zero, and can't even try, but we *can* divide by one. This means that although "can something come from nothing?" is incoherent and should not be asked, "can something come from something?" is quite valid, and has the possible result that "something" is its own answer. Ultimately, when the cause or source of the cosmos gets down to the simplest brute fact—when the divisor finally shrinks to one—the question will be "what is something divided by one?" The answer will be "itself." Since believers think "God divided by one" is a valid question while "God divided by zero" is not, why do they not allow me to think the same of the cosmos?

There actually is a sneaky way to do an end run and "divide by zero" without causing a crash, and that is to divide zero by itself. This is a trick because we can't actually divide by zero, and would never need to, but based on the axiom that any number divided by itself (n/n) is 1, we might logically (not mathematically) conclude that 0/0=1. This checks out because 1x0=0. So if 0/0=1, then "nothing from nothing" equals something. Something from nothing. If nothing truly existed (0/0), it would be something.

This is not a useless trick. The imaginary number *i* does not exist in reality. It is the square root of -1, which is impossible and incoherent. However, it can appear in an equation if it cancels itself out, such as in an oscillating electrical formula where the concept (not a real-world measurement) balances and disappears. The term "i/i" contains elements that make no sense on their own, but is useful precisely because it resolves to 1.

Since we do have evidence of the cosmos, and no evidence or coherent definition of a spirit, then which is more likely to be the numerator when the denominator gets to one? Which is more likely—the known cosmos or the unknown god—to be the something that doesn't have to come from anything?

What Is Evidence?

> *No one has ever seen God.*
> *—John 1:18*

Many of my debate opponents agree with me that there is actually no evidence for a god. If there were, we would not be having the debate. No one would be asking, "Why is there something rather than nothing?" because there would be better ways to argue. If there were truly evidence for a god, they would put it on the table. By now someone should have won the Nobel Prize for pointing out such evidence.

A few debate opponents actually do try to offer evidence: fulfilled prophecy, biblical foreknowledge of modern scientific findings, historical and contemporary miracles, "changed lives," answers to prayer, and the resurrection of Jesus. But if we scratch beneath the surface, as I have done in *Godless* and in *Losing Faith in Faith,* and many others have done elsewhere, these are easily dismissed. Since there is no real evidence, most debaters resort to "how do you explain *that?*" arguments, which are just various examples of the god of the gaps. They give evidence for current gaps or disagreements in scientific knowledge—such as the origin of the first living cell or replicating molecule, or the cause of the Big Bang, or the low likelihood of the initial physical constants possessing the precise values to allow for a universe with life,[28] or the astronomically low odds of an amino acid forming by blind chance, or the supposed inexplicability of what appear to be "irreducibly complex" features of the cell—curiously ignoring the fact that those gaps are what *drive* science (and some of those gaps are already closed)—but they never offer evidence *for* the god itself that supposedly closes those gaps. Evidence for a gap is not evidence for a god. They simply assert that their god hypothesis (or presupposition, as some theists honestly phrase it) is the best explanation for our current lack of knowledge. This is an argument from ignorance, not evidence.

Granting the lack of evidence, some believers come back with the brilliant parry: "Absence of evidence is not evidence of absence." So there! Since we atheists cannot absolutely prove that their supernatural god does not exist, they can pretend to be justified in maintaining their belief in what *might* be true, what is true to them by faith or presupposition. But, then, since no one can prove to me that leprechauns do not exist, can I assert that they do? Look at a box of Lucky Charms! If the absence of evidence is not evidence of absence, can you argue that I should stop believing in leprechauns? Of course you can. The absence of evidence is not *proof* of absence, but it is certainly *evidence* of absence. Absence is not a thing, but evidence of absence definitely is a thing. You can hold it in your hand.

Suppose during one of my debates—perhaps while we are discussing evidence—one of the organizers were to rush to the stage and announce that there was a bomb threat, advising us all to exit the building. We would hurry outside, a safe distance from the building, waiting while the police and experts do their job. After a while, suppose that the authorities announce it was just a hoax, that a thorough search of the building had been conducted and no bomb was found. They tell us it is now safe to enter the building. Would you go back in? I probably would. I think most of us would go back. We would have little fear because we would possess the assurance of the bomb experts that the building is clean.

But what would we actually have? Do we have proof that the bomb does not exist? No. But we do have evidence that the bomb does not exist. We have the results of the search. I presume that the experts would have moved methodically from room to room, opening drawers, boxes, and closets, looking in trash cans, under desks, behind curtains and vents, etc., applying their experience and training. Perhaps they used dogs to sniff for explosives, or that special tape that picks up minute particles of chemicals. I suppose they would produce a diagram or chart of the entire building and check off each location searched. When finished, that chart, indicating an absence of evidence, would be evidence of absence. You could hold it in your hand. It would be enough to convince you and me to go back into the building. It is not proof, but absence of evidence is indeed evidence of absence.

If something truly does not exist, the only possible evidence for its nonexistence would be the absence of evidence for its existence where we should expect it to be. Richard Dawkins points out in *The God Delusion* that "a universe with a God would look quite different from a universe without one." So far, conducting a comprehensive scientific search of the structure of the universe—certainly more thorough than any bomb squad—the chart has come up empty. We have evidence that God does not exist. We don't have proof, but it is safe to go back in the building.

Why are theists free to say leprechauns do not exist but atheists are not free to say the same about God? Well, because they believe in God and not in leprechauns. When Anselm concluded his famous ontological argument, thinking he had neatly proven the existence of God using mere words (which truly is something from nothing), he couldn't resist making a prayer with a jab at us nonbelievers: "Why, then, has the fool said in his heart, there is no God (Psalms 14:1), since it is so evident, to a rational mind, that you do exist in the highest degree of all? Why, except that he is dull and a fool?"[29] If anybody was dull, it was Anselm. I won't call him a fool, though he was certainly rude in spite of his intelligence. I think most believers are kinder than Anselm and would never stoop to name-calling or hurl insults, like the bible does, in order to belittle opposition or score a rhetorical point against atheists. I think most honest believers who truly wrestle with definitions and assumptions can admit that we atheists are just as committed to clarity as they claim to be. We disagree, but disagreement is not a crime. If more believers would respect the motives of atheists, wouldn't that be something, from nothing?

5

LIFE IS LIFE

That it will never come again is what makes life so sweet.
—Emily Dickinson

You are an ant carrying a bit of sand from one place to another. You are extremely light sensitive, and above ground you don't have much of a view of the world around your little sphere of activity, but you know how to get where you are going. Pheromones are your window to reality—smell is your worldview. As a worker ant, you spend your day sniffing around, bringing dirt, sand, or pebbles to the surface, toiling with hundreds of determined but clueless siblings to construct a mound. The mound is just a by-product of your efforts to move earth, but it becomes an object of its own. Nobody is in charge, but eventually your combined efforts result in a structure above and below ground that you can't picture but ends up protecting your colony so that the royalty can continue to breed, passing genes very similar to yours to the next generation, which will carry on just as you do. An instinct makes you and your coworkers drop a large pebble over an opening

161

that smells different from your own colony, smothering the enemy ants, though you don't know what you did or why you did it. You eat plant material, but are unaware of the fact that you would starve if not for the bacteria in your gut digesting your food. Your little brain is kept busy doing what you can't help doing. You never stop to contemplate the big picture.

Your colony is on the side of a dry riverbed in a deserted area rarely visited by other animals, but you don't know that. An occasional bird drops by, and you may sense its shadow darkening the ground as it flies off. Even with poor vision, a few photons that have bounced off the distant moon register on your tiny brain, though you don't know what that means. Perhaps, among the quadrillions of ants on our planet, your brain is a smidgen more intelligent—an Eentsy Einstein—and for a couple of seconds while munching on a leaf you actually think about something other than the daily grind for survival. You briefly recall the bird's shadow, the light from the round object in the sky, or part of the shape of the edifice you didn't know you were building. You can't visualize the structure the way the bird saw it, but you might think, "Hmmm. Something is there. What does it have to do with me? What are we doing? What is it all about?" Necessity pulls you back to your job, and you may feel a tiny twinge of hymenoptera pride as you dutifully live out the "meaning of life," struggling to serve your Sovereign. You don't know where you came from. You don't know how long your colony has been on that riverbank. You don't even know it is a riverbank. As far as you know, things have been like this forever and always will be.

Then a flash flood roars down the canyon and washes it all away. None of your instincts tells you what to do, except maybe "swim, swim, swim," if you are lucky enough to be above ground. Most of your co-workers drown and in a few seconds the entire colony is destroyed. Your civilization is wiped out.

The next day the lonely bird flies back over the sodden spot and sees that the anthill is gone. It glides further down the muddy riverbed and spots you, wandering alone, doing the only thing you know how to do, smelling around, moving some dirt. What if the bird were to yell down, "Stop it! It's pointless. Your queen is dead. Nobody cares, don't you see? You're wasting your time. Nothing lasts forever." Would you say, "Oh, sorry," and just give up? Or would you say, "I am an ant. What else am I supposed to do?"

Would your life have meaning?

I have talked about purpose in this book, but so far have said little about meaning. Are they the same? Is asking "what is the meaning of life?" the same as "what is the purpose of life?" As with purpose, would the reply be that there is no meaning *of* life but plenty of meaning *in* life? I think so, but with a subtle difference. Meaning and purpose are not the same thing. Meaning comes before purpose. The relationship between meaning and purpose is like the relationship between ethics and morality: it is the difference between theory and practice. Ethics and morality deal with behavior while meaning and purpose deal with intention. Meaning is the "theory" and purpose is the "practice" of intentionality.

Ethics and meaning deal with what we think about intentional actions abstractly (or theoretically), but morality and purpose deal with the actions themselves. In both cases, theory turns to practice at the point of intention. Instead of "theory and practice" we could say "planning and execution" or "conceptual and actual," but however we phrase it, it all hinges on intention. You can think and plan (ethics and meaning) all you want, but until you decide (intention) to put those ideas into action, you are neither moral nor purposeful.

Remember how I defined morality in chapter 2: the way to be moral is to act with the intention of minimizing harm. Minimizing harm is the theory, acting is the result of intention, and morality is the practice (or the post-judgment of the practice). Ready, set, go. Theory, intention, practice. Planning, intention, execution. Ethics, intention, morality. Meaning, intention, purpose. (I mean purpose in its primary usage, from inside a living being.)

You might possess a lofty moral philosophy or express wonderful creative concepts, but until you actually act in the real world, there is no way to judge your character or your ideas. It's a cute cliché to ask, "You can talk the talk, but can you walk the walk?" But before you can walk any walk, you have to know what the talk is saying. What does it *mean*?

Meaning, in its basic sense, is an idea, or information, that can be passed from one living thing to another, either by being intentionally communicated and acted upon, or by being read and discerned. It can be anything you can hold in your head: "liberty and justice for all," the color puce, how to make a machine accomplish a task, how to avoid danger, or a feeling like "I'm hungry." When someone speaks (or makes any intentional expression, such as in art or music), the listener or viewer tries to grasp what idea was intended to be conveyed from one mind to another, if any. If successful, the listener or observer has gone back in time, understanding what was in the mind of the speaker before the thought was expressed, and then reproduces those thoughts in the present in his or her own mind, to some degree of accuracy. Since they reproduce, meaningful thoughts can be like genes, as Richard Dawkins pointed out when he coined the word "meme." Successful communication (or meme replication) is not just a blind copying of nonsense syllables. It is knowing the meaning of what another mind intended to convey. It doesn't have to be stored as rote memory. When you tell a joke or funny story that you learned from someone else, you don't normally parrot the exact words from perfect recall. You usually rephrase it in your own words, perhaps changing a detail or embellishing here and there, but delivering the punch line with the same delicious incongruity that you appreciated when you first heard it.

When you look at a painting, you are gazing back into the mind of an artist. The artist likely didn't know you, but you can "read" the meaning, or try to. Visual or poetic art doesn't always have a "message"—what is conveyed can be simply a feeling, such as simple joy or despair, or beauty for the sake of beauty, or even ugliness for the sake of social commentary—but it does have intentionality. Art doesn't always have a point.

Well, pointillism does have a point, many points, though none of the points has a point in itself. Suppose you close your eyes and walk up to a huge pointillistic painting that you have never seen before, your nose almost touching the canvas. You open your eyes. You would see a few dots of color in front of your face. You could stare at one of the dots and ask, "What does it mean?" All by itself, that dot doesn't tell you anything. (The point is pointless.) It is no more artistic than a tiny coffee stain on your white shirt. But as you step back, knowing that as you move you will eventually "see" into the mind of the artist— and that is pretty exciting, knowing that you *will* see something—the dots lose their individual identity and merge together to create colors in your mind that may not actually appear on the canvas. The larger forms take shape, and suddenly you see a Sunday afternoon in the park. You see the big picture. That is what the artist intended. That is the "meaning" of the painting.

My brothers Tom and Darrell used to play in the high-school marching band. They not only paraded in rank-and-file formation, but they also performed complicated patterns that made shapes like a football, star, or the word "WIN," visible to the spectators in the stands. It didn't matter if they actually knew what they were doing—the instructions for forming the American flag might simply have been titled "Pattern #44" with directions like "right/left/about face/red card." The person who wrote those instructions had an intention of conveying a meaning to the crowd, and the execution was performed through the mechanism of (usually) coordinated musical students. Tom and Darrell had an intention and a purpose, though the meaning of their actions originated from and landed in someone else's mind. Each step they took, except for the proximate purposes of keeping them from falling and bumping into other players, had no meaning in and of itself.

Some believers might think this is a perfect analogy for the god they believe exists. We humans don't see the big picture, they say. Only the mind of God knows what it is all about. If we simply follow orders and march as we are directed, we can trust that the "meaning of life" will be seen from the Heavenly Bleachers when we rise above it all in the next life. But this misses the point that art is a medium. Art and language are not a beginning or an end (Alpha or Omega). The dots on the canvas are not the viewers of the painting. The dots, the marchers in the band, the ants in the colony, the words in a sentence, the notes in the melody, are all coming from one mind and aimed at another. If God is using us to convey a "meaning," then who is he talking to? Are people and ants just piano keys that God plays to amuse himself?

In the case of the dots on the canvas and the marchers in the band, we do know there was a human designer, but in the case of life itself we do not know that. In fact, we now know that life is the result of impersonal evolution and is not intelligently directed or designed at all. Since it *looks* designed—since natural selection utilizing randomness is not intuitively grasped by our minds—we (some of us) make the mistake of imagining there was an intelligent meaning behind it all.

I think all this talk about the "meaning of life" is just a way to pretend that our lives are validated. We don't want to feel pointless. We want a stamp of approval, or a sense that our activities are directed by and pointing to something larger than ourselves. We don't want to be mere dots on a canvas that could burn up, or ants that get washed away in a flash flood. We want to feel big, or a part of something bigger than just us, little us.

There is a silly scene in the movie *Pee-wee's Big Adventure* where Pee-wee loses control and falls off his bicycle in front of a crowd of children. As he stands up he says, "I meant to do that." That is very funny, but why? Because intention indicates meaning. It might also give dignity, depending on how you value bike-handling skills. What Pee-wee meant by "meant" (the meaning of meaning) was planning followed by intention followed by execution (hopefully followed by praise, or at least not ridicule). The humor in that scene comes from knowing that he was desperately trying to back engineer the process, saving face by making it appear that the accident was deliberate. He was attempting to instill meaning where there was none.

And so it is with life itself. I think the same impulse is behind our desire to seek the so-called meaning of life. Life, in the cosmic picture, is an accident. A bike wreck. A bike wreck that we survive and walk away from. It has no ultimate meaning. But that doesn't mean it is a mistake. It means it is the result of impersonal random processes, not intelligent planning. It didn't have to be. We didn't have to evolve. But we find ourselves here—like Pee-wee standing up after the crash—trying to save face. To give our lives some dignity, many say "it was meant to be," and a religious or transcendent explanation magically pops into existence—a deity, or arrangement of the stars, or complex cycle of reincarnation, or a journey to Vedic moksha, or a cosmic consciousness, or technologically advanced aliens experimenting in our galaxy, or a futuristic matrix, or the love of the Virgin Mary, or "principalities and powers" struggling over the souls of humankind.

We laugh when Pee-wee says "I meant to do that," but why don't we laugh when believers say "God gives meaning to my life"? We just hate to think the bird was right and there is no point to it all.

But what if that is exactly the case? What if there is no point? Wouldn't *that* be something worth knowing? Wouldn't *that* be worth our awe and admiration? Look at the beauty and dignity that have come from randomness! Since life is an accident, should we tell all the forgotten dead generations who came before us that they were wasting their time living their lives? (Most of those generations lived during a span of at least a hundred thousand years before Judaism, Christianity, and Islam.) Are we so insecure that we can't take our own lives as their own measure, their own reward? If you answer "Yes" to that question, you will be inclined to be religious; if you answer "No," you are a courageous human being.

Why does life have to have a point? If there were a point, then whatever makes the point would itself need a point. If whatever makes the point has a point, then whatever makes *that* point would have no point in itself. And so on. Eventually we have to come to a place where we stop asking, "What is the point?" and just start accepting life for what it is. If there is a god, he (she/it) would be in the same situation. He would have to say something like, "My life is my life, and that is that," with no further explanation, no ultimate meaning. Why can't we do the same thing, simply accepting the good fortune of being alive? Life is not only beside the point, it is above and beyond the point. It is precisely when we realize that there is no point, that we should not *want* there to be a point, that we can smile and say: "Life is life."

The word "life" also has the two usages of theory and practice. One conception of "life" is the mechanical differential survival of successful replicators due to natural selection. The other usage of "life" is the intentionality within any of the biological replicators themselves (you and me). Life as theory is evolution, and life as practice is intentionality (usually related to solving survival problems). So in the big picture, the reason you are here is evolution. The "theory of evolution" is the theory of life; it doesn't just scientifically explain the origin of species: it gives life its overall meaning (definition). Although meaning resides within a mind, it doesn't have to originate in a mind. If meaning is "an idea, or information, that is intended to be acted upon or communicated," as I said above, then it can arise from an impersonal process, as long as the transmission or discerning of the information is done by a living organism. Information resides not only within minds: it is also encoded in the genes. Plants pass "meaning" to the next generation, not from mind to mind but from life to life, as genetic information that allows them to grow, compete, survive, and reproduce in their particular environment.

As an organism with a brain, your own personal genes have survived partly due to decisions made within the minds of your ancestors, so in a sense, you have inherited the "thoughts" of your ancestors—not directly, but consequentially coded in the "last will and testament" they left behind in their germ cells, much like the inheritance of a real will tells you something about the intentions of your deceased ancestor. (The money came from them, but you get to spend it.) With sexual reproduction, when DNA is shuffled and copied from one generation to the next, information has been passed from two living beings to another. Every cell in your body contains "meaning" from your ancestors. (I put "meaning" in quotes because it is just information that is passed. It becomes meaning when we think about it.) Your ancestors were not talking directly to you, but like an artist, they created a product that speaks to the future.

Your birth was a happy accident, for you at least, and probably also for the two people who mixed their DNA to produce you. You are here because your biological parents had sex (or your parental germ cells were brought together in vitro), and they were only able to do so because their parents had had sex, and so on, back through the "shadows of forgotten ancestors," as Carl Sagan and Ann Druyan phrased it. It is not called a "sex drive" for nothing. Your great-grandparents were real-life biological phenotypes "driven" by the selfish genes they carried, yet those genes care about nothing. The genes survive only because they are good at surviving and replicating. (Actually, they code for proteins that do the work.) The same is true with you. Genes do not care about you; they only appear to care about themselves. (That is why Richard

Dawkins calls them "selfish genes," although he is careful to warn that using a teleological phrase to describe impersonal random processes is simply employing a figure of speech. Those genes are not "caring" about anything at all: they only work "as if" they had intentionality or internal purpose, and to our designing minds, this is a useful metaphor.) The genes you carry are there simply because they were successful in making copies—the survival of the fittest—which in our species means surviving long enough to find a mate, give birth, and nurture those babies to adulthood where they can do the same. In that sense, the "meaning of life" (the meaning of the word "life") is an impersonal mathematical model, the ruthless statistical filter of natural selection through which your genes have managed to pass. From the point of view of the genes, your body is simply an environment, a lumbering jury-rigged Rube Goldberg vehicle built of proteins struggling to carry those genes to another generation. The "fittest" get copied while the less fortunate go extinct.

But the other usage of "life"—the practice, not the broad theory—refers to the phenotype (an individual organism, such as you, the expression of a genotype), which is your own body and brain, constructed by genes to contain instincts, unique attributes, behavior, and feelings, all to marshal your genes to another generation. From *your* perspective, the bird's-eye view of the phenotype, it looks like you have personal meaning and purpose, or many meanings and purposes—you want, feel, love, hate, and aim your energies in certain directions—but this is not the "meaning of life." If you insist on attaching a "meaning" to what is happening, in a broad sense, then don't think about yourself: think about the past and the future, the flow of evolution. Think about those genes of yours—or closely related genes, if you are childless—that may appear way down the line, many generations from now as the "meaning" you have here right now. But we don't have to think of "meaning" at all. We can just be happy living our lives, aiming at our immediate goals, and if in the process we happen to intend to do something, and then do it, then we have purpose, and that is what we meant to do. That is the meaning *in* life.

Thinking about future genes is not reincarnation. Our genes live on, but our individual personalities die with our unique bodies. Many of the American Indian tribes had a cyclical model of time, as did other groups around the globe, and I think there is some value to that model, though I see it as a wheel that is rolling forward, not stationary like a water wheel. (Sometimes it rolls "backward," as in the case of parasites or wingless birds who are simpler than their ancestors.) I think each generation of humans can be thought of as a turn of the wheel, and it is rolling "forward" in the sense that since DNA is recombined, shuffled between two parents, it is not spinning in place like it would be if each copy were identical. (The shuffling actually happens between your grandparents' DNA, which your parents pass on to you in two sets of chromosomes. Your parents' DNA gets shuffled when *you* produce germ cells to pass on.)

I had eight great-grandparents, like virtually everybody else,[1] and what a mix they were! None of those eight people originally knew that their genes would end up in *me*, a future descendant, and only one of them actually learned that fact. I have inherited from each of them, statistically, about one eighth of the genes that make me different from everyone else. I know something about only six of them, since my Mom never knew her father and her mother never said much about him, if he indeed was her father, a man from Texas named Swenson (who we think was married) who got Grandma pregnant when she was fifteen. Grandma's Dad, my great-grandfather John Elmer Sopher, died in the 1918 "Spanish flu" epidemic. His mother was a tiny Chiricahua Apache (so I'm Geronimo!) named Isabel Camacho who was born in Hermosillo, Mexico (so I'm Mexican!). I have a photo of my five-year-old mother standing with her wizened great-grandmother Isabel.

(Mom looks like a happy Shirley Temple, who was born the same year she was.) Isabel was a feisty, independent woman rumored to smoke a corncob pipe, roll her own cigarettes, and lived to be ninety, quite an accomplishment in those days. John Sopher's father Winfield might have been a Marrano (or Converso),[2] one of those cryptic Jews who had fled Spain and were pretending to be Catholic. (So I'm Jewish!) The name Sopher is Hebrew for "scribe," and here I am, scribing. His wife Angelita, the one great-grandparent whom I did meet, could speak Spanish, owned and ran the Spanish Kitchen restaurant in Tucson, but boasted that her Spanish was from Spain, not Mexico (though her mother was born in Veracruz, Mexico). She usually called herself Angelina or Angeline instead of Angelita, because it sounded more European. Her daughter, my grandma Alice Edith Sopher, also spoke a limited Spanish, but it sounded like childish Mexican street talk that she must have picked up when she was growing up in Tucson. (She was actually born in a boxcar.) I think I owe my existence to that 1918 flu epidemic that killed her father, aunt, and little sister. My Mom was born out-of-wedlock to the sixteen-year-old Alice who, according to Grandma Angelita and the uncles who ended up raising her little girl, had become something of a wild child looking for love after her beloved Daddy was killed by that flu. (Hence, the uncertainty of Mom's paternity, although from my point of view her birth was not "illegitimate" at all.)

On my Dad's side I know a lot more. I learned just a little about his mother's Cherokee and French grandparents, but thanks to the fact that his father, a Delaware Indian (or Lenape, the real name of our tribe), was quite a storyteller, we have a fuller picture of the paternal side of the family, as recounted in his memoirs, *Paradise Remembered*.[3] In the introduction to the book, *Legends of the Delaware Indians and Picture Writing*, by Richard C. Adams, I found this historical note:

On April 27, 1904, a general council of the Delaware tribe met at Dewey, Indian Territory, to assess the status of their claims against the government and to vote on the proposed settlement of those claims. . . . The council elected a committee of eleven men to discuss the issues and make a recommendation. These eleven men, who represented some of the leading families of the tribe, were: Stephen Miller, Jim Wilson, Simon Secondine, Charley Elkhair, William Smith, Arthur Armstrong, Jack Barker, John McCracken, John Kinney, Tom Lane, and John Willey."[4]

My great-grandfather is in that list. Jack Barker, my Dad's grand-dad, was part of that historic committee that voted to define the Delaware Tribe as "the 985 Registered Delawares on the Pratt Roll of 1867, taken in Kansas, and their living descendants." That 1867 census had happened when about half the tribe left the reservation in Kansas to move to Indian Territory, which became part of Oklahoma in 1906. (Those who stayed in Kansas assimilated. You can see the Delaware tribal seal on the tiled floor of the Kansas City airport.) Current membership is based on the 1906 payment roll. Jack was basically voting to ensure that his wife Lizzie, who was born a granddaughter of chief Captain Ketchum (so I'm royalty!) on the Kansas reservation, and their children, would be official members of the tribe, as recognized by the Lenape as well as the U.S. government. His son Herbert (my Granddad, whose tribal name was My Friend) was almost nine years old at the time of that council and, according to Adams, was a child in one of the "leading families of the tribe" residing in Indian Territory (so I'm nobility!). Well, the tribe was less than 1,000 people then and there, so it wasn't hard to be a leading family.[5] This was after seven historical migrations that almost drove our tribe extinct, starting with the infamous 1737 Walking Purchase (in New Jersey/Pennsylvania along the Delaware River, after which the Lenape tribe was named by the Europeans), a purported contract between the Delaware and the Penn family that resulted in our first expulsion. (We are a very smart tribe. We sold Manhattan to the Dutch for $24.) We later passed through seven different states, leaving our mark in each one, before being given the choice between assimilation and resettlement from the reservation in Kansas (because the railroad was constructed through there) to Indian Territory in 1867. My great-grandmother Elizabeth ("Lizzie") Wolf was five years old when her family chose to travel with the chief south to a strange new land. We were forced to live alongside the Cherokees and other tribes who had arrived via their own trail of tears. Jack Barker was actually not born a Delaware Indian. His mother was a Cherokee and his father was probably English. They moved to Indian Territory in 1874 when he was seventeen, seven years after Lizzie's family arrived, and when he married the full-blood Lizzie in a Delaware ceremony, he became a full Delaware himself, and hence all their children, including my Granddad, were full members of the tribe. Since little Herbert Barker, born in 1895, is named in those tribal rolls and U.S. government documents (the Dawes roll), my brothers and I and our cousins and children are today all full voting members of the tribe. I just mailed a tribal ballot during the writing of this chapter.

By the way, if you ever eat in the Mitsitam Café in the National Museum of the American Indian in Washington, DC, you should know that *mitsitam* is the Lenape word for "let's eat." I don't know if there is any significance to this, but when Linda LaScola (Daniel Dennett's colleague), Elisabeth Cornwell (of the Richard Dawkins Foundation for Reason and Science), and I decided to get together in January 2011 to discuss how we might help ministers and priests who no longer believe to leave the ministry, we met in that museum. The Clergy Project was born in the Mitsitam Café.

I can understand why John Curtis ("Jack") Barker was elected to that committee. He was smart and industrious. I saw a photograph of him with a rifle in one hand and a science magazine in the other (with a modern train engine on the cover). I can picture Lizzie and Jack meeting and falling in love in that lush land. My grandfather related many tales about his family, including stories that his parents told about *their* parents, stories we are very fortunate to have. The picture he paints is not what you might expect of a bunch of natives living in wild Indian Territory before statehood. He describes the two-story house they built in the country south of Welch, complete with piano, spacious yard trimmed with a lawnmower, surrounded by solid rock walls (I have a stone from part of the front gate), orchards, gardens, large barn, cattle and horses, smokehouse, icehouse, and slaughterhouse. Their property was often visited by members of the Lenape and Cherokee community, as well as by members of other tribes and non-Indians who availed themselves of their generosity. When some of the poor white "Sooner" settlers were passing through the area, they sometimes knocked on the doors of the relatively rich Indians, asking for a handout. (All of this changed when oil was discovered in northern Oklahoma and we lost our land, by hook or crook.) It was obvious that Granddad deeply loved and admired his parents. His memoirs wistfully recount those years of hard work and happiness.

My ancestors, like yours, were survivors. Even if I didn't know about my great-grandparents, I have inherited "meaning" from them. My Granddad relates their difficulties, especially the immense struggles his parents happily endured to raise a large family. One of the most harrowing incidents was when he nearly died from appendicitis when he was seventeen. Lizzie spotted her son crawling down the dirt road toward the house in horrible pain. They rushed in a wagon, every bump in the road a torture, to the railroad tracks near Welch where they flagged down a train that took him, his Dad, and the doctor to a hospital hours away in Kansas City, every vibration on the ride an agony of pain. The police would not let them off the train for a while because there had been a robbery in town. It was my Granddad's first visit to a city, and when they finally got to the hospital, he was confused when they appeared to waste time, rolled him into a little room and did nothing, then rolled him back out again—a country boy's first experience with an elevator. Jack, always science minded, stood by the doctor and watched the entire operation and later described it all in graphic medical detail. Those doctors back in 1912 did a decent job, or I wouldn't be here writing about it.

I know your own family history has fascinating stories, just as interesting, but I'm telling you all of this to make a point. (There *is* a point!) The living, loving, vibrant Jack and Lizzie Barker had purpose-filled lives, though they never had an image of their great- and great-great-grandchildren in their minds. (Now they have great-great-great-grandchildren, including ten grandkids of my own.) They certainly hoped that their many sons and one surviving daughter would have children someday, but they died before my Granddad got married, so my Dad never knew them, nor they him.[6] All those years of changing diapers, tending fields and cattle, constructing buildings, teaching the kids how to hunt and fish, growing and cooking food, mending clothes, engaging in business and travel, serving as a deputy sheriff, chasing outlaws (one actually had a peg leg), chopping ice, butchering hogs, playing with the children, swimming in Barker Hole in Little Cabin Creek, singing songs, and telling jokes and stories—all of that busy activity, for what? Like the ants by the riverbed, they are dead and gone, and if it had not been for me and Grandma preserving the memoirs of one of their children, they would be completely forgotten. I doubt that any of my children have given them much thought, and why should they? Unless you happen to be one of the rare genealogists or historians, the lives of your ancestors have little immediate impact on your daily life—except for the amazing fact that every cell in your body contains genes that came directly from those people.

At one level, I am their life, though they didn't know about me at all. The "meaning of life" in the broad sense (in the theory sense, the definition, the theory of evolution) is entirely different from the "meaning in life" up close. And the same is true in the other direction. If any of my future descendants happen to know about me, they might muster an acknowledging "thanks," but then get back to their own struggles, their own happiness, their own meaning. Knowing this might have happened someday long after they were dead—that their great-grandson would love to say to them, "Thank you for all you did"—Jack and Lizzie might have stopped for a second to say, "You're welcome," but then, like the busy ant, got back to work.

Suppose that pessimistic bird (or its ancestor) were to have flown over the home that Jack and Lizzie built, saying, "Stop it! What you are doing is pointless. Your life, your house, your children and grandchildren will all be forgotten. The cosmos doesn't care. A flash flood will destroy it all. There is no meaning to any of this." Even if true, would they have stopped? Of course not. Humans do what humans do. My great-grandparents John and Angelita and Jack and Lizzie (from different diasporas) led meaningful lives, in both senses, from *their* point of view as well as mine. Even if they had had no grandchildren—and some people indeed lead meaningful childless lives by choice, enhancing and protecting the lives and genes of others—their life would have been their life, and that is beautiful all by itself.

You are lucky if you happen to have memoirs from past generations, but most of your ancestors are truly forgotten. I love this little essay by Robert Green Ingersoll, the great nineteenth-century agnostic orator. It is called "After Visiting the Tomb of Napoleon."

> A little while ago I stood by the grave of Napoleon, a magnificent tomb of gilt and gold, fit almost for a dead deity, and gazed upon the sarcophagus of black Egyptian marble where rests at last the ashes of the restless man. I leaned over the balustrade and thought about the career of the greatest soldier of the modern world.
>
> I saw him walking upon the banks of the Seine contemplating suicide; I saw him at Toulon; I saw him putting down the mob in the streets of Paris; I saw him at the head of the army of Italy; I saw

him crossing the bridge at Lodi with the tricolor in his hand; I saw him in Egypt in the shadows of the pyramids; I saw him conquer the Alps and mingle the eagle of France with the eagles of the crags. I saw him at Marengo, at Ulm and Austerlitz. I saw him in Russia, where the infantry of the snow and the cavalry of the wild blast scattered his legions like winter's withered leaves. I saw him at Leipsic in defeat and disaster, driven by a million bayonets back upon Paris, clutched like a wild beast, banished to Elba. I saw him escape and retake an Empire by the force of his genius. I saw him upon the frightful field of Waterloo, when chance and fate combined to wreck the fortunes of their former king. And I saw him at St. Helena, with his hands crossed behind him, gazing out upon the sad and solemn sea.

I thought of the orphans and widows he had made; of the tears that had been shed for his glory and of the only woman who had ever loved him pushed from his heart by the cold hand of ambition.

And I said I would rather have been a French peasant and worn wooden shoes. I would rather have lived in a hut with a vine growing over the door and the grapes growing purple in the kisses of the autumn sun. I would rather have been that poor peasant with my loving wife by my side, knitting as the day died out of the sky, with my children upon my knee and their arms about me. I would rather have been that man and gone down to the tongueless silence of the dreamless dust than to have been that imperial impersonation of force and murder known as Napoleon the Great.

And so I would ten thousand times.[7]

I had a similar feeling when I visited the cliff dwellings at Walnut Canyon, southeast of Flagstaff, Arizona. About 100 people had lived there, 800 to 900 years ago, and it must have been beautiful. I sat for a while in one of the caves that the original inhabitants fortified, gazing at the canyon wall on the other side, the greenery from the river below and the bright sky above. I wondered who else had been sitting in that same spot centuries ago, perhaps a mother singing to her baby, or a young woman watching a sun-tanned young man climbing on the other side, or a grandfather gazing at the stars. I looked up at the ceiling that had been blackened by smoke from ancient fires and tried to imagine what was going through the minds of those nameless and forgotten people who might have descendants among us. My first thought is to say that we don't know what they were thinking. But on the other hand, we *do* know what they were thinking. They were human beings, just like us, with the same instincts, feelings, desires, hopes, and rational minds. They were survivors. They may be forgotten, but their lives were not meaningless.

Just a couple of weeks before turning in the manuscript to this book, I stood on the top of the massive Sun Pyramid in Teotihuacán, Mexico. Gazing down at the long Avenue of the Dead, flanked by temples, leading to the smaller (but just as impressive) Moon Pyramid in the distance, I tried to picture the people who built those structures. Thousands of individuals and hundreds of families lived in that now-deserted city. Some of them must have been standing in exactly the same spot where I was, gazing down at their friends and relatives populating the area. After so many centuries of existence, long before the pre-Columbian Aztecs arrived to claim the area, there must have been lovers meeting on the sides of that pyramid. I imagined them looking down at their world, promising their futures, starting their new families. As a group, they were obviously very superstitious, maybe even religious fanatics. But as individuals, they must have been just like you and me. If they had not built those temples, would we have even known of their existence?

We can keep going back in time to the early Mayans, Chinese, Romans, Greeks, Egyptians, the original Paleoamericans, Australian aborigines, way back to the Cro-Magnons, earlier to the related Neanderthals, and even much earlier to the human primates Australopithecus afarensis ("Lucy")—and these are just a few of the groups that we know about. We know that anatomically modern humans arose in Africa and spread out from there. (So we could not have originated in the Middle Eastern "Garden of Eden.") For more than

100,000 years since then, all those lives and families, increasing population, diverging into "races," languages, cultures, territorial conflicts, most not knowing of each other, hundreds of generations passing, lovers meeting, babies raised, wounds nursed, homes constructed, tools built, food gathered and prepared, music performed, faces painted, jewelry crafted, dances danced, deaths grieved, cultures and civilizations rising and disappearing—most of it obliterated. What, exactly, was that all about? Were they struggling to bring "glory to God," or were they simply living? Not knowing about Moses, Jesus, or Muhammad, were their lives wasted? Like the ant colony destroyed by a flash flood, was it all meaningless?

My Mom died in 2004 when she was seventy-six years old. She never got old, but she had to die anyway. I say she never got old because her mind was always childlike, in the good sense. She was curious, creative, and happy. She laughed and sang, planted beautiful gardens (she turned the Arizona desert into a real Garden of Eden), solved puzzles, made up word games, told jokes, and played pranks. She had a beautiful singing voice, an undiscovered Shirley Temple, and later an undiscovered Ella Fitzgerald. She met my Dad in a 1940s band—she was the singer and he played trombone. Less than five feet tall, she was always "little Patsy" to her family, having been raised mainly by her grandmother and uncles, and she was often more like a little sister to us three growing boys. She was not simple-minded—she was very smart—but she was simple-hearted. She had a sign in her kitchen: "I'm only in it for the love." At the last moment in the hospice, when she had had enough suffering and voluntarily pulled out the tube, she couldn't speak but turned and stared into Dad's dark eyes as if to say, "Thank you for a wonderful life." A legitimate life.

My Dad has still not gotten over her. None of us has. She still lives in our minds. Although Mom had been a Sunday School teacher and raised us boys as fundamentalist Christians, she died an atheist. She eventually realized, as I did, that *this* life is the only life that matters. Dad, also now an atheist, knowing I had been a minister and could conduct services, asked me to say some words at Mom's graveside at Mountain View Cemetery in Mesa, Arizona. That was one of the hardest things I have ever had to do, emotion struggling with speech, acting the officiant at my own mother's memorial. I wanted to find words that honored her life yet were not disrespectful to those who had come to the service, including many family members who remain devout believers. "Mom did not believe in life after death," I said. "She believed in life before death." A couple of relatives grumbled at those comments, but they could not argue with the fact that those were *her* views and that she was indeed an amazing woman, a good atheist. "Although Mom did not believe she would live on in a transcendent world," I continued, "she knew that she would live on in the memories of those of us who remain, and in the lingering effects of the deeds she did while alive. In that very natural sense—in the happy optimistic genes she bequeathed to us three boys and in the work she did to educate us, improve and beautify the world—she does live on."

My mother loved country music. When she entered the hospital for what we didn't know was the last time, I told her I had written a song just for her, in a country style, thinking it would give her something to look forward to, to hang on. I should have taken a guitar there a couple of weeks earlier and sung it directly to her, but I unwisely decided to wait until the song was properly recorded. I had the CD professionally produced, all ready to play for her, but she died a few minutes before I got on the plane. She never heard this song.

"None of the Above"

Everybody tries to tell me
I need to choose a god to love,
But after looking them all over,

I'll take none of the above.
I am happy in the natural world,
Like a hand fits in a glove.
Only sinners need a savior.
I'll take none of the above.

Why talk to me of heaven?
What makes you think I wanna go,
When it's right here in the real world
Where the milk and honey flow?

You preachers and messiahs,
What were you thinking of?
Don't need to fix what isn't broken.
I'll take none of the above.[8]

I thought about playing that song during the memorial service—I had the CD in hand—but I knew Mom would not have wanted her relatives and friends to feel uncomfortable, so I put it back in my pocket. My brother Tom, still a born-again believer (and a good man), asked if we could include a moment of silence. I thought that was a wise idea. It allowed those who were believers to pray quietly, not openly dismissive of Mom's views yet giving them a chance to grieve in their own way. At that moment, Tom walked over and placed his hand on Mom's casket with eyes closed. He and I do not share the same views, but we do share the same loss.

If that nihilistic bird had flown over the scene saying, "See! It's all pointless," I would have looked up and said, "Speak for yourself." As the mocking creature flew away, I would have yelled, "You didn't know my Mom."

Our daughter Sabrina had a bird once, a cockatiel named Pikachu, and that little creature was definitely not nihilistic. Cockatiels are intensely social animals, and this one craved interaction. It's amazing how such a tiny brain can produce so much personality. That bird became a member of the family. He would feed from his own bowl at the dinner table each night, joining in the conversation, bobbing his head and "talking" in his bird-like way. He would say Sabrina's name when he heard her coming down the stairs, and he sang a specific song when he saw me, as if to say, "Hi, Dan." He could recite the words of the poet Christina Rossetti, "My heart is like a singing bird." When we came into the house, we usually greeted him by name, so eventually when he heard us opening the door, he would say, "Pikachu!" He wanted to be held and talked to and groomed. In the mornings, watching me approach the windows, he would mimic the sound of the shades rising before I pulled the cords. I think that is amazing. It puts birds not in a separate class of specially created creatures, but on a continuum of intelligence with all other animals, including humans. Pikachu never did recognize himself in a mirror—he would posture to fight the male intruder—so his theory of mind was less than ours, but it was not zero. He was definitely a distinct personality.

Sabrina invented a word for this. When she was in her early teens, she started calling Pikachu a "zird." When he did something funny or smart, she would say, "You're a good zird!" I asked her what she meant by that, and she said that calling him just a "bird" was not enough to describe what he was, as if he were an alien. (She says it was because when he repeated "Good bird!" it sounded like "Gud zird.") To her, to all of us, that creature was a part of the family with a unique personality and should not be insulted by being classed as qualitatively inferior. A "zird" is a person, any person, not just a human animal. Sabrina would sometimes call *me* a zird, and I took it as a compliment. If you have a close friend who is a cat, dog, or other animal, you have a zird—well, you don't *have* a zird, because you can't own another person, but you have a friend who is a zird. Legally, Sabrina owned Pikachu, but in reality they were two separate persons, different species linked by a real friendship. Zirds of a feather.

When Pikachu died suddenly one spring morning when he was only eight years old (I think he had hit his head the night before while flying across the room), it was a death in the family. We made a little cardboard casket and buried him by the daffodils. Sabrina wrote on the casket: "My heart is like a singing bird."

Those would have been perfect words for my Mom's casket.

I doubt that Pikachu ever sat around wondering "what is the meaning of life?" From what I could see, he was curious, exploratory, interactive. He would listen to sounds, turn his head, and sometimes reproduce those sounds. When he spoke Sabrina's name or sang that melody for me, I think there was a meaning to it. He was not engaging in a full language conversation, but he was producing sounds that "meant" something. (Well, he probably didn't know what we thought it meant. I had his cage out on the front porch one day when a woman walked by the house and Pikachu made the very loud "cat-call" whistle. The woman turned and glared at me.) Sabrina thought he had free will, as much as any of us have free will (which may not be much, if at all), and I don't know about that, but I do know he had intentionality. His mind intended to produce an expression or action, for whatever reason, and that shows purpose. Zirds have meaning in life, or they wouldn't be zirds. The fact that that little creature still lives in our minds, and now in the pages of this book, means that something very meaningful happened that affected us all. Pikachu is dead, but I can describe that zird to you, using words.

What is a word? It is a symbol. It is a basic unit of meaning, a group of sounds or characters that intend to communicate an idea from one mind to another. A word does not represent itself—it stands for something else: an object, an action, a person, a quality, a concept. This is proved by the fact that different languages have different words for the same things. But if a word is a symbol for something else, what does the word "word" mean? Since a word is a symbol, "word" is a symbol for a symbol. Is there a word for *that* concept, for a word or phrase that is two steps away from reality? Wittgenstein talked about the fact that all technical language is a "symbol for a symbol," and algebra is like that, using letters to stand for variable numbers that measure something else. Since I can't find a single word to represent that concept, let's do what Sabrina did and make one up. If I had asked Pikachu for a "good word" for the concept, he might have said "gud zord." Let's call a symbol for a symbol a "zord." (Rhymes with zird.) The word "word" is a zord.

The "meaning *in* life" comes from a mind knowing or learning something it wants to communicate or act on—and Pikachu certainly did that—but the "meaning *of* life" is a zord. It is an empty zord, a concept for a concept without referent. It doesn't point to anything in the real world. Pikachu didn't need it, and neither do you. Since meaning comes *from* life, not the other way around, asking for the meaning *of* life is like asking for the life of life. Meaning is within the mind; the mind is not within meaning. The only zirds who find a zord like "the meaning of life" useful are philosophers and theologians, and even philosophers (who can recognize themselves in a mirror) now dismiss the question as passé and naive. (And since theology is a subject with no object, it has nothing meaningful to say about it.) We can indefinitely stack symbols upon symbols, concepts upon concepts, reaching up to an infinite God or down to nothingness, but it is all a trick of language. If it doesn't ultimately refer to anything real, it is vacant vocabulary. "In the beginning was the Zord, and the Zord was with God, and the Zord was God," the gnostic evangelistic John tells us in his first sentence. But what does that mean? A zord can be useful (like the word "word"), but only if it ultimately refers to something that actually exists—a referent to which the symbol of the symbol can point. At the end of the day an algebraic equation has to resolve to so many apples or kilometers, or it is just make-work. The "meaning of life" never resolves to anything real, but the "meaning in life" certainly does.

Do you want meaning? Then learn something.

There is a scene in the musical movie *Camelot* where King Arthur realizes his life is falling apart and he goes to Merlin for advice. "What should I do?" he asks in desperation. Merlin turns to Arthur and says, "Learn something." I think that is wonderful advice, even from the lips of an actor playing a fictional wizard that I don't believe could exist speaking to a legendary king who may not have existed. I have often told my kids, "If you are not learning, you are not living."

I love the subtitle of Dan Dennett's book, *Darwin's Dangerous Idea: Evolution and the Meanings of Life.* That is "meanings" plural. There is no single meaning of life, but there are many ways for life to have meaning. I take Dan's "meanings of life" to be the same as "meaning in life." It comes from inside life, not outside. It is bottom-up, a crane, not a skyhook. It comes from variety, messiness, randomness, and struggle within the natural world, not from some pristine, perfectly holy mono-meaning in the clouds.

Would you like the world to have meaning? Then create something. Speak, write, sing, compose, sculpt, build, paint, dance. You be the creator.

Do you want purpose? Then do something. Solve a problem. "After all is said and done," Aesop said, "more is said than done." Take what you have learned (meaning) and turn it into action (purpose).

Just like the ant colony, someday a flash flood will destroy the human race. It might come as a rain of asteroids, or worse, a rain of our own missiles. It might be a killer virus, or burst of lethal cosmic rays tearing through the ozone layer. If we manage to prevent or escape those catastrophes, there is no denying the fact that our sun will expand to a red giant in about five billion years (so we are halfway there), either totally enveloping and incinerating the earth or, at minimum, mercilessly boiling away all water, sterilizing the planet of life. Perhaps some of our descendants will have figured out how to flee the solar system, but in the bigger picture, there is no escaping the eventual big crunch or big freeze of the universe we inhabit. At that final point of our unavoidable destiny, there will be no Mockingzird in the Sky, no "Zord of God" calling down "I told you so." It will all be over and forgotten—and since there will be no one left to do the forgetting, it will be truly unforgettable. Do you find that depressing? I find it exhilarating.

In the movie *Annie Hall* by Woody Allen, nine-year-old Alvy has stopped doing his homework, so his mother takes him to a psychiatrist who asks, "Why are you depressed, Alvy?"

"Well, the universe is everything," Alvy says, "and if it's expanding, someday it will break apart and that would be the end of everything! . . . What's the point?"

"What has the universe got to do with it?" his mother asks. "You're here in Brooklyn! Brooklyn is not expanding!"

Alvy and his mother are both right. There is no meaning in the cosmic picture, but there is meaning in the here and now. Here in Brooklyn.[9] How do you feel about that? What can you do about it? You already know that your not-too-distant descendants will forget about you, or even if they don't—even if you become astonishingly famous and remembered for millennia—your life will be mere memories in *their* minds. Your mind will be gone, as will theirs someday. Should you stop doing your homework? Should you throw down your napkin in nihilistic despair? When you think about all of the possible catastrophes that could wipe out the human race, one of which *will* occur, or all of the potential dangers to you and your loved ones, don't you have an urge to protest, to escape, to fight back, to keep living? Don't you love your family, your species, your animal cousins, your planet?

That is life. Like the surviving ant, you can't help it. Life is life. Life, by definition—by necessity—protects and cherishes itself.

Suppose the red-wing blackbird, chirping from the top of the fencepost, were actually saying: "I am the king of this fencepost! Look at me! I was designed to be beautiful and important. This fencepost, this road, these fields were all created so that I could exist." That's what creationists think: "The universe was fine-tuned for us, us, us." They are narcissistic. They are looking through the telescope the wrong way, imagining it all points back to "me, me, me." That is not theology—that is me-ology.

It is only when you realize that nothing matters on the cosmic scale when you can decide what really matters. Since the cosmos doesn't care, you must care.

The ant colony is gone. The ancient Egyptians are gone. The original Mayans and Aztecs are gone. The Walnut Canyon Indians are gone. Napoleon is gone. Jack and Lizzie are gone. John and Angelita are gone. Little Patsy is gone. It doesn't last forever—and that's what makes it so sweet! You and I who were lucky enough to be born get to enjoy the ride. Do not die to yourself. Don't blow your one and only shot at happiness by selling your birthright and squandering your meaning and purpose on someone else's undeserved glory. Live your own life. If you are reasonable and kind, you will discover that meaning is not handed to you from on high; it emerges naturally from your own life-driven purpose.

ACKNOWLEDGMENTS

I want to thank those who generously gave of their time to read all or parts of the manuscript of this book, or to help me wrestle with concepts during the writing. *Life Driven Purpose* could not have been what it is without their insights, criticisms, and suggestions. They include: Philip Appleman, Darrell Barker, Geoff Carr, Rodger Clark, Scott Colson, Jerry Coyne, Richard Dawkins, Jason Eden, Andrew Gaylor, Annie Laurie Gaylor, Sabrina Gaylor, Justin Johnson, Buzz Kemper, David Lambourn, Linda LaScola, Lisa Lee, David Lintner, Lon Ostrander, Gricha Raether, Keith Robertson, Andrew Seidel, Vic Stenger, Phil Stilwell, Gary Thompson, and Larry Thomson. And thank you, Kurt Volkan, for believing in this book.

NOTES

Chapter 1: The Good News

1. Psalm 14:1, Psalm 53:1. One of my favorite quips is, "The fool says in his heart 'There is no God,' but the wise man says it out loud." See also footnote 16 to chapter 4.

2. Enjoyment is mainly a result, not an aim. I think enjoyment is a measure of the success of our efforts. But since our bodies evolved pleasure circuits—the opposite of pain—to actually feel good when our purposes are met, those feelings themselves can be something to aim for. Pleasure for the sake of pleasure. I think that is partly how evolution works. By following instincts to satisfy our drives toward pleasure, we are prodded toward survival. Why do we want to feel good? "Duh! Because it feels good." But I think feeling good is a sign that everything is okay, an indication that we have succeeded, a proof that we are alive. The fact that some humans seek shortcuts to pleasure—such as thrill seeking, drugs, sexual experimentation, and other riskier activities—does not mean that pleasure evolved as an end in itself. Nor does it mean that pleasure for its own sake is bad; it is the risk that is bad, not the pleasure. In any event, some of us find immense enjoyment in the simple fact that we have reached a goal we were aiming for. Full enjoyment won't happen if the aim of purpose is not met. (I am assuming that most of us are mentally healthy. I don't know if sociopaths, psychopaths, or self-destructive individuals actually enjoy their actions, but they are a small slice of humanity. I talk about how we judge behavior in chapter 2.)

3. 2 Corinthians 4:7

4. Romans 12:1–2

5. Galatians 2:20

6. Philippians 1:21

7. Luke 9:23

8. *Warren v. Commissioner of the Internal Revenue* 302 F.3d 1012, 9th District federal court. See Erwin Chemerinsky, "The Parsonage Exemption Violates the Establishment Clause and Should be Declared Unconstitutional," (2003), Duke Law Faculty Scholarship, Paper 737. See also Jon Wiener, "Rick Warren's Clout," *The Nation*, February 2, 2009.

9. The Freedom From Religion Foundation has sued the IRS over this violation of the First Amendment. On November 22, 2013, a federal judge ruled in our favor, declaring the parsonage allowance exclusion to be an unconstitutional preference for religion. This finding, if upheld, will affect more than a half million clergy in the United States. The government will most certainly have appealed that decision by the time this book is published.

10. Philippians 1:21

11. Luke 9:23

12. Rick Warren, *The Purpose Driven Life: What On Earth Am I Here For?* (Zondervan, 2002). These quotes also appear in the abridged booklet, Rick Warren, *What On Earth Am I Here For?* (Zondervan, 2004).

13. Ibid.

14. 1 Corinthians 6:20

15. 1 Corinthians 10:31

16. 2 Corinthians 10:5

17. Matthew 5:16

18. Galatians 1:10

19. Revelation 4:11

20. From the American Declaration of Independence, which reads in part: "But when a long train of abuses and usurpations, pursuing invariably the same Object evinces a design to reduce them under absolute Despotism, it is their right, it is their duty, to throw off such Government, and to provide new Guards for their future security.—Such has been the patient sufferance of these Colonies; and such is now the necessity which constrains them to alter their former Systems of Government. The history of the present King of Great Britain is a history of repeated injuries and usurpations, all having in direct object the establishment of an absolute Tyranny over these States." (The words "them" and "their" refer to "the people.")

21. I first read it phrased like this by philosopher Kai Nielsen: "If there is no God, it is indeed true that we are not blessed with the questionable blessing of being made for a purpose; furthermore, if there is neither God nor *Logos*, there is no purpose to life, no plan for the universe or providential ordering of things in accordance with which we must live our lives. Yet, from the fact, if it is a fact, that there is no purpose to life or no purposes for which we are made, it does not at all follow that there are no purposes *in* life that are worth achieving, doing, or having, so that life in reality must be just one damn thing after another that finally, senselessly terminates in death. . . . In a Godless world, in which death is inevitable, our lives are not robbed of meaning." Kai Nielsen, *Ethics Without God* (Prometheus Books, 1990)

22. The Clergy Project was started in 2011 for precisely that purpose, to help ministers, priests, and rabbis who no longer believe to land on their feet. Daniel C. Dennett and Linda LaScola write about this problem in their article titled "Preachers Who Are Not Believers," *Evolutionary Psychology* 8, no. 1 (2010), www.epjournal.net/filestore/EP08122150.pdf. The Clergy Project, a private online forum for ministers, priests, and rabbis who are now atheists or agnostics, can be found online at http://clergyproject.org

23. I wrote a song called "My Father's House," in a defiant rock style, for the Freedom From Religion Foundation's CD, *Beware of Dogma*. The lyrics include these words: "But now that I have grown, it's time to use my own good mind. I'm outa here! Let me outa here! I found my own place—I've left my father's house behind."

24. Joel Osteen, *Your Best Life Now: 7 Steps to Living at Your Full Potential* (FaithWords, 2007).

25. Here is the fuller quote from Craig: "If there is no God, then man and the universe are doomed. Like prisoners condemned to death, we await our unavoidable execution. There is no God, and there is no immortality. And what is the consequence of this? It means that life is absurd. It means that the life we have is without ultimate significance, value, or purpose." See William

Lane Craig's chapter titled "The Absurdity of Life without God" in *Reasonable Faith* (http://www.reasonablefaith.org/the-absurdity-of-life-without-god).

26. You can read my summary of that debate, "This House Does Not Believe in God," in the November 2012 issue of *Freethought Today*. Videos of the event are online (www.youtube.com/watch?v=btJazTimH4M). At the end of the event, Oxford Society president John Lee announced to the audience that they were to "vote with your feet." Those in favor of the proposition ("This house believes in God") were to exit the room by one door, and those in favor of the opposition were to exit by a different door. After counting the people passing through each door, the results were announced at the post-debate reception: 143 for the proposition, and 168 for the opposition. The atheists won! That 54–46 percent result was greater than president Obama's popular vote in the U.S. election the same week.

27. Jayant V. Narlikar, "An Indian Test of Indian Astrology," *Skeptical Inquirer*, March/April 2013.

28. Genesis 3:7

29. Profiles of hundreds of other influential atheists and agnostics can be found on the Freedom From Religion Foundation's "Freethought of the Day" webpage at http://ffrf.org/news/day. An anthology of the writings of more than 50 female freethinkers (including Elizabeth Cady Stanton and Margaret Sanger) can be read in Annie Laurie Gaylor, *Women Without Superstition: "No Gods—No Masters" (The Collected Writings of Women Freethinkers of the Nineteenth and Twentieth Centuries)* (FFRF, 1997).

Chapter 2: Mere Morality

1. The name of the cricket in the Disney movie *Pinocchio* was probably picked because "Jiminy Cricket" (mangled from "Jiminy Christmas") was originally a substitute minced oath for "Jesus Christ," the words having the same initials. The Romans used to swear to the god Gemini, and Christians who later wanted to curse but did not want to "take the Lord's name in vain," could say "Gemini Christmas" instead of "Jesus Christ!" ("Jeepers Creepers" is another example.) Further evidence that the Disney writers meant to subtly identify Jiminy Cricket with Christianity are the lyrics paraphrasing Jesus:

"Take the straight and narrow path and if you start to slide, give a little whistle."

2. C. S. Lewis, *Mere Christianity*. In spite of Lewis's valiant attempt to unite Christians, they continue to fight about what should be considered nonessential doctrines, so his argument is moot, persuasive only to a subset of believers. In the chapter "Mere Assertions" in *Losing Faith in Faith*, I analyze Lewis's moral argument. In *Godless*, I discuss his famous trilemma—"Jesus was either a lunatic, liar, or Lord"—pointing out that he ignored a fourth option: legend.

3. Daniel C. Dennett, *Intuition Pumps and Other Tools For Thinking* (W. W. Norton, 2013).

4. Humanism as a philosophy and way of life is broader than that, but humanistic morality is concerned mainly with harm, as measured against human needs and values. The American Humanist Association has this definition: "Humanism is a progressive philosophy of life that, without theism and other supernatural beliefs, affirms our ability and responsibility to lead ethical lives of personal fulfillment that aspire to the greater good of humanity." The Humanist Manifesto III, talking about "want," "cruelty," "violence," "brutality," and "suffering," contains these words about morality and meaning: "Ethical values are derived from human need and interest as tested by experience. Humanists ground values in human welfare shaped by human circumstances, interests, and concerns and extended to the global ecosystem and beyond. We are committed to treating each person as having inherent worth and dignity, and to making informed choices in a context of freedom consonant with responsibility. Life's fulfillment emerges from individual participation in the service of humane ideals. . . . Humanists rely on the rich heritage of human culture and the lifestance of Humanism to provide comfort in times of want and encouragement in times of plenty. Humans are social by nature and find meaning in relationships. Humanists long for and strive toward a world of mutual care and concern, free of cruelty and its consequences, where differences are resolved cooperatively without resorting to violence. . . . Working to benefit society maximizes individual happiness. Progressive cultures have worked to free humanity from the brutalities of mere survival and to reduce suffering, improve society, and develop global community. We seek to minimize the inequities of circumstance and ability, and we support a just distribution of nature's resources and the fruits of human effort so that as many as possible can enjoy a good life. Humanists are concerned for the well being of all, are committed to diversity, and respect those of differing yet humane views. We work to uphold the equal enjoyment of human rights and civil liberties in an open, secular society and maintain it is a civic duty to participate in the democratic process and a planetary duty to protect nature's integrity, diversity, and beauty in a secure, sustainable manner."

5. "But he said unto them, All men cannot receive this saying, save they to whom it is given. For there are some eunuchs, which were so born from their mother's womb: and there are some eunuchs, which were made eunuchs of men: and there be eunuchs, which have made themselves eunuchs for the kingdom of heaven's sake. He that is able to receive it, let him receive it." Matthew 19:11–12

6. Robert A. Burton, MD, *On Being Certain: Believing You Are Right Even When You're Not* (St. Martin's Press, 2008).

7. Letter to Thomas Law, June 13, 1814. Notice that Jefferson did not say "God hath implanted in our breasts a love of others," or "we have been endowed by our Creator with a certain unalienable love for others." Jefferson lived his life as what we might call a "practical atheist," not believing in a personal deity but (as a pre-Darwinian freethinker) assuming there must have been a creative force that started it all, most often equating "God" with "nature."

8. Charles Darwin, *Descent of Man*, chapter 3.

9. Marc Bekoff and Jessica Pierce, "The Ethical Dog," *Scientific American Mind*, March/April 2010. The authors discover that canids indeed know how to "play fair," following principles we would call "moral": (1) communicate clearly, (2) mind your manners, (3) admit when you are wrong, (4) be honest. "Violating social norms . . . is not good for perpetuating one's genes," the authors write.

10. Acts of cruelty against other animals are well-known danger signs. Sociopaths, psychopaths, and abusers often escalate from hurting nonhuman animals to hurting human beings. These people are off to the far side of the bell curve. I don't know if this is due mainly to genetics or illness, but I suspect it is a mixture of both.

11. I don't believe in a soul or spirit. The word "soul," as a transcendent entity, has never been defined, so it points to nothing real. If atheists ever use the word, we usually put it in quote marks and consider it a synonym for something like personality or emotion, which are purely natural. See chapter 4, "Much Ado About," for more discussion of "spirit."

12. Jerry Coyne, *Why Evolution Is True* (Oxford University Press, 2009).

13. Bernd Heinrich, *The Mind of the Raven* (Cliff Street Books, 1999).

14. Jeremy Bentham, *The Constitutional Code* (1830).

15. There is a difference between descriptive laws and prescriptive laws. The laws of nature are descriptive. The laws of society are prescriptive. To say that the laws of society originate in minds is not to say that the laws of nature must also originate in a mind.

16. I actually know something about this. My Dad was an Anaheim Police officer for more than twenty years, and while I was in high school I accompanied him to "Skid School" at the station. We studied the coefficients of various road surfaces, related to their type (concrete, asphalt, grass, gravel, dry or wet, etc.), how to estimate the speed of a vehicle at the point when the driver hit the brakes and started skidding across those surfaces (depending on weight and orientation), and how to locate the point of impact from reading skid marks of multiple vehicles before and after impact. The most common thing Dad heard at the scene of an accident was, "I didn't see the other car."

17. I remember hearing Johnny Carson tell a joke on *The Tonight Show* years ago: in California you can rob a bank and shoot the security guards while leaving the building, but when crossing the street be careful not to jaywalk! (Paraphrased from memory.)

18. I haven't been able to obtain the recording as of the time of this writing, so I'm paraphrasing from memory.

19. I discuss the inadequacies of the Ten Commandments in depth in *Godless*.

20. Jefferson wrote: "For we know that the common law is that system of law which was introduced by the Saxons on their settlement in England, and altered from time to time by proper legislative authority from that time to the date of Magna Charta, which terminates the period of the common law, or lex non scripta, and commences that of the statute law, or Lex Scripta. This settlement took place about the middle of the fifth century. But Christianity was not introduced till the seventh century; the conversion of the first christian king of the Heptarchy having taken place about the year 598, and that of the last about 686. Here, then, was a space of two hundred years, during which the common law was in existence, and Christianity no part of it. . . . If, therefore, from the settlement of the Saxons to the introduction of Christianity among them, that system of religion could not be a part of the common law, because they were not yet Christians, and if, having their laws from that period to the close of the common law, we are all able to find among them no such act of adoption, we may safely affirm (though contradicted by all the judges and writers on earth) that Christianity neither is, nor ever was a part of the common law." Thomas Jefferson, "Whether Christianity Is Part of the Common Law?"

21. John F. Kennedy, a Roman Catholic, under accusations that if elected president his allegiance would be more toward Rome than Washington, gave a famous campaign speech to the Greater Houston Ministerial Association in 1960, in which he uttered these famous words: "I believe in an America where the separation of church and state is absolute; where no Catholic prelate would tell the President—should he be Catholic—how to act, and no Protestant minister would tell his parishioners for whom to vote; where no church or church school is granted any public funds or political preference, and where no man is denied public office merely because his religion differs from the President who might appoint him, or the people who might elect him. I believe in an America that is officially neither Catholic, Protestant nor Jewish; where no public official either requests or accept instructions on public policy from the Pope, the National Council of Churches or any other ecclesiastical source; where no religious body seeks to impose its will directly or indirectly upon the general populace or the public acts of its officials, and where religious liberty is so indivisible that an act against one church is treated as an act against all."

22. When Thomas Jefferson was working on the Declaration of Independence, he smudged out a word and replaced it with the word "citizens." It wasn't until recently that scholars were able to use a hyperspectral camera in the Library of Congress to separate out several layers of ink on his draft to read the word underneath. The word he replaced was "subjects." Jefferson had started his draft by copying from the Virginia Constitution (which he had written two months earlier), but then obviously reconsidered what he wanted to say. I think that little smudge was a huge turning point in the history of freedom and democracy, and Jefferson's deliberate rejection of "subject" tells us what was on his mind. We Americans are under no authority but "We, the people." We are not subjects of a king, master, or Lord. Steve Marsh, "The World's Memory Keepers," *Delta Sky Magazine*, 2012.

23. I point out the logical flaws, question begging, and equivocations in William Lane Craig's Kalam Argument in my "Cosmological Kalamity" chapter in *Godless*.

24. See William Lane Craig's chapter titled "The Absurdity of Life without God" in *Reasonable Faith* (http://www.reasonablefaith.org/the-absurdity-of-life-without-god).

25. Transcribed from "William Lane Craig on Dan Barker and Sam Harris," YouTube, on May 24, 2010, www.youtube.com/watch?v=aQ7C6SVrUjw.

26. For documentation of the Lenape heritage in Manhattan, see, for example, Evan T. Pritchard, *Native New Yorkers: The Legacy of the Algonquin People of New York* (Council Oak Books, 2002).

27. The claim that the biblical god is a "moral monster" has been most recently made by Hector Avalos, especially in his chapter "Is Yahweh a Moral Monster?" in John W. Loftus's edited volume *The Christian Delusion* (Prometheus Books, 2010), but also in his own book, *Fighting Words: The Origins of Religious Violence* (Prometheus Books, 2005).

28. Romans 3:23

29. Romans 3:12. The bible assumes that "sin" is a meaningful wrong, a crime against God. The Greek word for "sin" is *hamartia,* which means "to miss the mark," or to fall short of God's holiness. Since there is no God, it follows that there is no such thing as sin.

30. Romans 6:23

31. 1 Corinthians 15:22

32. See, for example, Phil Zuckerman, *Society Without God* (New York University Press, 2010).

33. The Trolley Problem was introduced by Philippa Foot in 1967. It was also analysed by Judith Jarvis Thomson, Peter Unger, and Frances Kamm.

Chapter 3: Religious Color Blindness

1. Bill Maher on stem cells from his HBO stand-up comedy special titled ". . . But I'm Not Wrong" (www.facebook.com/video/video.php?v=116716561681913).

2. Gregory J. Riley, *The River of God: A New History of Christian Origins* (Harper Collins, 2001).

3. John W. Loftus, *The Outsider Test for Faith: How to Know Which Religion Is True* (Prometheus Books, 2013).

4. Stanford Rives, *Did Calvin Murder Servetus?* (BookSurge Publications, 2008). Lawrence Goldstone and Nancy Goldstone, *Out of the Flames: The Remarkable Story of a Fearless Scholar, a Fatal Heresy, and One of the Rarest Books in the World* (Broadway Books, 2002).

5. Bart Ehrman, *Did Jesus Exist?: The Historical Argument for Jesus of Nazareth* (HarperOne, 2012).

6. Richard C. Carrier, *Proving History: Bayes's Theorem and the Quest for the Historical Jesus* (Prometheus Books, 2012).

7. The back cover of Ehrman's book says, "The Jesus you discover here may not be the Jesus you had hoped to meet—but he did exist, whether we like it or not."

Chapter 4: Much Ado About

1. Winston Churchill, *My Early Life: 1874–1904* (Thornton Butterworth, 1930), chapter III.

2. Many misuse the phrase "beg the question." A reporter might write, "The inconclusive investigation begs the question: Where is the murder weapon?" when the reporter really means the investigation *raises* or *prompts* the question. "Begging the question" is something different. It is a fallacy in formal logic that assumes the truth of a conclusion within the very argument itself, with reference to nothing else outside of the argument. Such an argument is circular, which is what happens when the conclusion shows up in one of the premises before the conclusion is even reached.

3. "I Got Plenty o' Nothin'," from the 1935 musical *Porgy and Bess* by George and Ira Gershwin.

4. Lyrics from John Lennon's "Strawberry Fields Forever," 1967.

5. Bertolt Brecht, *Mother Courage and Her Children: A Chronicle of the Thirty Years' War* (1939).

6. K. C. Cole, *The Hole in the Universe: How Scientists Peered over the Edge of Emptiness and Found Everything* (Mariner Books, 2001).

7. Lawrence M. Krauss, *Quintessence: The Mystery of Missing Mass in the Universe* (Basic Books, 2001).

8. Samuel Beckett, *Watt* (Grove Press, 1959).

9. Imaginary numbers are useful in equations only when they cancel themselves out. No final solution can be the square root of a negative number. If nothingness is like an imaginary number, then it has to cancel itself out.

10. Frank Wilczek, "Cosmic Asymmetry," *Scientific American*, December 1980. "Why is there anything at all, and not rather nothing? Because nothing is unstable."

11. Lawrence M. Krauss, *A Universe From Nothing: Why Is There Something Rather Than Nothing* (Free Press, 2012), page 153.

12. This is the famous Hawking radiation. Astrophysicist Victor Stenger wrote: "Quantum electrodynamics is a fifty-year-old theory of the interactions of electrons and photons that has made successful predictions to accuracies as great as twelve significant figures. Fundamental to that theory is the spontaneous appearance of electron-positron (anti-electron) pairs for brief periods of time, literally out of 'nothing.'" "The Other Side of Time," www.infidels.org/library/modern/vic_stenger/otherside.html (2000). Physicist Lawrence Krauss wrote: "The vacuum of modern particle theory is a strange place indeed. From an unchanging 'void' it has become an active arena out of which particles might be created or into which they might be destroyed. . . . The vacuum might even be the 'source' of all matter in the universe." Lawrence M. Krauss, *Quintessence: The Mystery of the Missing Mass* (Basic Books, 2001).

13. Lawrence M. Krauss, *A Universe From Nothing: Why Is There Something Rather Than Nothing* (Free Press, 2012), page 151.

14. Stephen Hawking and Leonard Mlodinow, *The Grand Design*, (Bantam, 2010).

15. From Brian Kolodiejchuk, M.C., ed. *Mother Teresa, Come Be My Light: The Private Writings of the Saint of Calcutta* (Doubleday, 2007).

16. I have simplified Anselm's ponderous ruminations for the modern reader. One translation from his *Proslogion* (1077–1078) puts it like this: ". . . And assuredly that, than which nothing greater can be conceived, cannot exist in the understanding alone. For, suppose it exists in the understanding alone: then it can be conceived to exist in reality; which is greater. Therefore, if that, than which nothing greater can be conceived, exists in the understanding alone, the very being, than which nothing greater can be conceived is one than which a greater can be conceived. But obviously this is impossible. . . . God cannot be conceived not to exist. God is that, than which nothing greater can be conceived. That which can be conceived not to exist is not God. And it assuredly exists so truly, that it cannot be conceived not to exist. For, it is possible to conceive of a being which cannot be conceived not to exist; and this is greater than one which can be conceived not to exist. Hence, if that, than which nothing greater can be conceived, can be conceived not to exist, it is not that, than which nothing greater can be conceived. But this is an irreconcilable contradiction. There is, then, so truly a being than which nothing greater can be conceived to exist, that it cannot even be conceived not to exist; and this being you are, O Lord, our God. . . . If a mind could conceive of a being better than you, the creature would rise above the Creator; and this is most absurd. And, indeed, whatever else there is, except you alone, can be conceived not to exist. To you alone, therefore, it belongs to exist more truly than all other beings, and hence in a higher degree than all others. For, whatever else exists does not exist so truly, and hence in a less degree it belongs to it to exist. Why, then, has the fool said in his heart, there is no God (Psalms 14:1), since it is so evident, to a rational mind, that you do exist in the highest degree of all? Why, except that he is dull and a fool?"

17. I further debunk the ontological argument in my book *Godless*.

18. From the movie *Without Feathers* (1975).

19. In *Godless*, I use members of an orchestra and items in the set of even numbers to illustrate this concept, but you can probably think of many examples yourself.

20. From a San Francisco comedy monologue, as quoted in Kathleen Tracy, *Ellen: The Real Story of Ellen DeGeneres* (Pinnacle, 2005), page 76.

21. The chapter "Cosmological Kalamity" in my book *Godless* debunks one version of the Kalam Cosmological Argument for the existence of God.

22. If a spirit can create matter, this would violate the first law of thermodynamics, the law of conservation, which says that matter can neither be created or destroyed. If believers counter that the laws of thermodynamics apply only to the natural world, then they should also stop using the second law of thermodynamics—which states that entropy ("disorder") increases in a closed system—in their other arguments that try to prove the supernatural.

23. Joel Osteen, *Your Best Life Now: 7 Steps to Living at Your Full Potential* (FaithWords, 2007).

24. Delos McKown is a former Baptist preacher who became an atheist, head of the Philosophy Department at Auburn University, and freethought author. I heard Delos make this statement in a public speech. It is also quoted in Victor J. Stenger, *Physics and Psychics: The Search for a World Beyond the Senses* (Prometheus Books, 1990).

25. Acts 2:1–4

26. The lyrics to the songs in *The Wizard of Oz* movie, including "Over the Rainbow," as well as some of the dialogue, were written by Yip Harburg, who was an atheist. My favorite light-verse poem of his is "Lead, Kindly Light": "Where Bishop Patrick crossed the street, An X now marks the spot. The light of God was with him, But the traffic light was not." (Poem available in *Rhymes For The Irreverent* [Freedom From Religion Foundation, 2006].)

27. As quoted in Joan Conner, *You Don't Have to Be Buddhist to Know Nothing*, (Prometheus Books, 2009), page 143. Dunham is a U.S. mathematician, professor, and author.

28. For an excellent refutation by a physicist of the "fine-tuning" argument, see Victor J. Stenger, *The Fallacy of Fine Tuning: Why the Universe Is Not Designed For Us* (Prometheus Books, 2011).

29. See footnote 16.

Chapter 5: Life Is Life

1. I say "virtually everybody else" because if your parents were first cousins, you do not have eight great-grandparents. Charles Darwin married his first cousin Emma Wedgwood, so their children had only six great-grandparents.

2. From an Arabic word meaning "forbidden," *marrano* was applied in Spain to the food that Muslims and Jews were forbidden to eat. It then became a pejorative for crypto-Jews (Jews pretending to be Christians) who preferred hypocrisy over death. Today, *marrano* is just another word for pig, with no religious connotations. *Converso* is less derogatory.

3. Herbert Barker, Sr., edited by Dan Barker, *Paradise Remembered: A Lenape Indian Childhood* (limited family publication by Dan and Marie Barker, 1991).

4. Richard C. Adams, introduction by Deborah Nichols, *Legends of the Delaware Indians and Picture Writing* (Syracuse University Press, 2000), pages xxxiii–xxxiv.

5. The book also says that about 1/4 of the tribe (200) were Christian, and about 1/4 were Delaware religion. The other half were apparently nothing at all.

6. Lizzie Barker's gravestone in Walker Cemetery, northwest of Welch, Oklahoma, shows "1860–1916," but the birth year is incorrect because the family bible had it wrong. The bible was corrected to 1862, but it was too expensive to correct the granite.

7. William Holden quotes part of this essay by Robert. G. Ingersoll to Judy Holliday in the 1950 movie *Born Yesterday*.

8. "None of the Above" is recorded on the Freedom From Religion Foundation's *Beware of Dogma* album.

9. Brooklyn was originally Lenape territory until we "sold" it to the Dutch. Brooklyn is the Anglicized form of the Dutch *Breuckelen,* named after a city in the Netherlands (Breukelen). The original Lenape name was Marechkawick ("fortified home"). So perhaps the reason Brooklyn is not expanding is because it was fortified by my ancestors?

BIBLIOGRAPHY

References and related reading, by chapter, alphabetical by author

Introduction

Ali, Ayaan Hirsi. *Infidel*. Atria Books, 2007.

Avalos, Héctor. *¿Se Puede Saber Si Dios Existe?* Prometheus Books, 2003.

Barker, Dan. *Losing Faith in Faith: From Preacher to Atheist*. Freedom From Religion Foundation, 1992.

Barker, Dan. *Godless: How An Evangelical Preacher Became One of America's Leading Atheists*. Ulysses Press, 2008.

Bloom, Howard. *The God Problem: How a Godless Cosmos Creates*. Prometheus Books, 2012.

Boghossian, Peter. *A Manual For Creating Atheists*. Pitchstone Publishing, 2013.

Christina, Greta. *Why Are You Atheists So Angry? 99 Things That Piss Off the Godless*. Pitchstone Publishing, 2012.

Dawkins, Richard. *The Blind Watchmaker: Why the Evidence of Evolution Reveals a Universe Without Design*. W. W. Norton, 1986.

Dawkins, Richard. *The God Delusion*. Houghton Mifflin, 2006.

Dennett, Daniel C. *Breaking The Spell: Religion as a Natural Phenomenon*. Penguin, 2006.

DeWitt, Jerry, with Ethan Brown. *Hope After Faith: An Ex-Pastor's Journey from Belief to Atheism*. Da Capo, 2013.

Edis, Taner. *The Ghost in The Universe*. Prometheus Books, 2002.

Grayling, A. C. *Against All Gods: Six Polemics on Religion and an Essay on Kindness*. Oberon Books, 2007.

Grayling, A. C. *The God Argument*. Bloomsbury, 2013.

Harris, Sam. *The End of Faith: Religion, Terror, and the Future of Reason*. Norton, 2005.

Hitchens, Christopher. *God Is Not Great: How Religion Poisons Everything*. Twelve, 2007.

Kick, Russ, ed. *Everything You Know About God Is Wrong: The Disinformation Guide to Religion*. Disinformation Company, 2007.

Krueger, Douglas E. *What Is Atheism? A Short Introduction*. Prometheus Books, 1998.

Lobdell, William. *Losing My Religion: How I Lost My Faith Reporting on Religion in America—and Found Unexpected Peace*. Harper, 2009.

Loftus, John W. *The Christian Delusion: Why Faith Fails*. Prometheus Books, 2012.

Loftus, John W. *Why I Became an Atheist: A Former Preacher Rejects Christianity*. Prometheus Books, 2012.

Loftus, John W. *The Outsider Test for Faith: How To Know Which Religion Is True*. Prometheus Books, 2013.

Mills, David. *The Atheist Universe: The Thinking Person's Answer to Christian Fundamentalism*. Ulysses Press, 2006.

Onfray, Michel. *In Defense of Atheism: The Case Against Christianity, Judaism and Islam*. Penguin Canada, 2007.

Paulos, John Allen. *Irreligion: A Mathematician Explains Why the Arguments for God Just Don't Add Up*. Hill and Wang, 2012.

Pinn, Anthony. *The End of God Talk: An African-American Humanist Theology*. Oxford University Press, 2012.

Sagan, Carl. *The Demon-Haunted World: Science as a Candle in the Dark*. Random House, 1995.

Sagan, Carl. *The Varieties of Scientific Experience: A Personal View of the Search for God*. Penguin, 2006.

Smith, George H. *Atheism: The Case Against God.* Prometheus Books, 1989.

Smith, George H. *Why Atheism?* Prometheus Books, 2000.

Stenger, Victor J. *God, The Failed Hypothesis: How Science Shows That God Does Not Exist.* Prometheus Books, 2007.

Stenger, Victor J. *The New Atheism: Taking a Stand for Science and Reason.* Prometheus Books, 2009.

Stenger, Victor J. *God and the Folly of Faith: The Incompatibility of Science and Religion.* Prometheus Books, 2012.

Sweeney, Julia. *Letting Go of God* (audio CD with booklet). Julia Sweeney, 2006.

Thomson, Jr., MD, J. Anderson, with Clare Aukofer, *Why We Believe in God(s): A Concise Guide to the Science of Faith.* Pitchstone Publishing, 2012.

Whittenberger, Gary J. *God Wants You To Be an Atheist: The Startling Conclusion From a Rational Analysis.* Outskirts Press, 2012.

Wolpert, Lewis. *Six Impossible Things Before Breakfast: The Evolutionary Origins of Belief.* Norton, 2008.

Zuckerman, Phil. *Faith No More: Why People Reject Religion.* Oxford University Press, 2011.

Chapter 1: The Good News

Barker, Dan. *The Good Atheist: Living a Purpose-Filled Life Without God.* Ulysses Press, 2011.

Beaumont, Paul. *A Brief Eternity* (fiction, with a philosophical/theological perspective). Dangerous Little Books, 2013.

Dennett, Daniel C. *Darwin's Dangerous Idea: Evolution and the Meanings of Life.* Touchstone, 1995.

Gaylor, Annie Laurie. *Women Without Superstition: "No Gods—No Masters" (The Collected Writings of Women Freethinkers of the Nineteenth and Twentieth Centuries).* Freedom From Religion Foundation, 1997.

Price, Robert M. *The Reason Driven Life: What Am I Here on Earth For?* Prometheus Books, 2006.

Chapter 2: Mere Morality

Avalos, Hector. *Fighting Words: The Origins of Religious Violence*. Prometheus Books, 2005.

Barker, Dan. *Maybe Right, Maybe Wrong: A Guide For Young Thinkers*. Prometheus Books, 1992.

Bentham, Jeremy. *The Constitutional Code*. 1830.

Bloom, Paul. *Just Babies: The Origins of Good and Evil*. Crown Publishers, 2013.

Coyne, Jerry. *Why Evolution Is True*. Oxford University Press, 2009.

Dennett, Daniel C. *Intuition Pumps and Other Tools For Thinking*. Norton, 2013.

Denonn, Lester E., ed. *The Bertrand Russell Dictionary of Mind, Matter & Morals*. Citadel Press, 1952. First Carol Publishing, 1993.

de Waal, Frans. *Primates and Philosophers: How Morality Evolved*. Princeton University Press, 2006.

Dugatkin, Lee Alan. *The Altruism Equation: Seven Scientists Search for the Origins of Goodness*. Princeton University Press, 2006.

Ehrman, Bart D. *God's Problem: How the Bible Fails to Answer Our Most Important Question—Why We Suffer*. Harper Collins, 2009.

Epstein, Greg M. *Good Without God: What a Billion Nonreligious People Do Believe*. William Morrow, 2009.

Gazzaniga, Michael S. *The Ethical Brain*. Dana Press, 2005.

Goldberg, Stuart C. *God On Trial 2000: Indictment of God for Crimes against Job*. PROSCOP, 1999.

Harris, Sam. *The Moral Landscape: How Science Can Determine Human Values*. Free Press, 2010.

Hauser, Marc D. *Moral Minds: The Nature of Right and Wrong*. Harper Perennial, 2006.

Heinrich, Bernd. *The Mind of the Raven*. Cliff Street Books, 1999.

Loftus, John W., ed. *The Christian Delusion*. Prometheus Books, 2010.

McGowan, Dale. *Parenting Beyond Belief: On Raising Ethical, Caring Kids Without Religion*. AMACOM, 2011.

Nielsen, Kai. *Ethics Without God.* Prometheus Books, 1990.

Pfaff, Donald W. *The Neuroscience of Fair Play: Why We (Usually) Follow The Golden Rule.* Dana Press, 2007.

Ridley, Matt. *The Origins of Virtue: Human Instincts and the Evolution of Cooperation.* Penguin, 1996.

Sinnott-Armstrong, Walter. *Morality: Without God?* Oxford University Press, 2009.

Smith, Tara. *Viable Values: A Study of Life as the Root and Reward of Morality.* Rowan & Littlefield, 2000.

Tremblay, Rodrigue. *The Code for Global Ethics: Ten Humanist Principles.* Prometheus Books, 2010.

Wielenberg, Erik J. *Value and Virtue in a Godless Universe.* Cambridge University Press, 2005.

Wright, Robert. *The Moral Animal: Why We Are The Way We Are: The New Science of Evolutionary Psychology.* Vintage Books, 1994.

Chapter 3: Religious Color Blindness

Barker, Dan. *Maybe Yes, Maybe No: A Guide For Young Skeptics.* Prometheus Books, 1990.

Boyer, Pascal. *Religion Explained: The Evolutionary Origins of Religious Thought.* Basic Books, 2001.

Burton, MD, Robert A. *On Being Certain: Believing You Are Right Even When You're Not.* St. Martin's Press, 2008.

Carrier, Richard C. *Proving History: Bayes's Theorem and the Quest for the Historical Jesus.* Prometheus Books, 2012.

Cohen, Edmund D. *The Mind of the Bible Believer.* Prometheus Books, 1983.

Dawkins, Richard. *The Extended Phenotype: The Long Reach of the Gene.* Oxford University Press, 1989.

Dennett, Daniel C. *Freedom Evolves.* Penguin Books, reprint, 2004.

Doherty, Earl. *The Jesus Puzzle: Did Christianity Begin with a Mythical Christ? Challenging the Existence of an Historical Jesus.* Age of Reason Publications, 2005.

Ehrman, Bart. *Did Jesus Exist?: The Historical Argument for Jesus of Nazareth.* HarperOne, 2012.

Goldstone, Lawrence, and Nancy Goldstone. *Out of the Flames: The Remarkable Story of a Fearless Scholar, a Fatal Heresy, and One of the Rarest Books in the World.* Broadway Books, 2002.

Hoffer, Eric. *The True Believer: Thoughts on the Nature of Mass Movements.* Harper & Row, 1951.

Loftus, John W. *The Outsider Test for Faith: How to Know Which Religion Is True.* Prometheus Books, 2013.

McCormick, Matthew S. *Atheism: And the Case Against Christ.* Prometheus Books, 2012.

McGrayne, Sharon Bertsch. *The Theory That Would Not Die: How Bayes' Rule Cracked the Enigma Code, Hunted Down Russian Submarines & Emerged Triumphant from Two Centuries of Controversy.* Yale University Press, 2011.

Riley, Gregory J. *The River of God: A New History of Christian Origins.* Harper Collins, 2001.

Rives, Stanford. *Did Calvin Murder Servetus?* BookSurge Publications, 2008.

Shermer, Michael. *The Believing Brain: From Ghosts and Gods to Politics and Conspiracies—How We Construct Beliefs and Reinforce Them as Truths.* Times Books, 2011.

Tarico, Valerie. *Trusting Doubt: A Former Evangelical Looks at Old Beliefs in a New Light.* Oracle Institute Press, 2012.

Chapter 4: Much Ado About

Carroll, Sean. *The Particle at the End of the Universe: How the Hunt for the Higgs Boson Leads Us to the Edge of a New World.* Dutton Adult, 2012.

Cole, K. C. *The Hole in the Universe: How Scientists Peered over the Edge of Emptiness and Found Everything.* Houghton Mifflin Harcourt, 2001.

Conner, Joan. *You Don't Have to Be Buddhist to Know Nothing.* Prometheus Books, 2009.

Hawking, Stephen, and Leonard Mlodinow, *The Grand Design.* Bantam, 2012.

Krauss, Lawrence M. *Quintessence: The Search For Missing Mass in the Universe.* Basic Books, 2001.

Krauss, Lawrence M. *A Universe from Nothing: Why There Is Something Rather Than Nothing.* Free Press, 2012.

Leuten, Kuenftigen. *The Meaning of Life the Universe and Nothing* (2 volumes). European Press Academic Publishing, 2011.

Stenger, Victor J. *Physics and Psychics: The Search for a World Beyond the Senses.* Prometheus Books, 1990.

Stenger, Victor J. *The Comprehensible Cosmos: Where Do the Laws of Physics Come From?* Prometheus Books, 2006.

Stenger, Victor J. *Quantum Gods: Creation, Chaos, and the Search for Cosmic Consciousness.* Prometheus Books, 2009.

Stenger, Victor J. *The Fallacy of Fine Tuning: Why the Universe Is Not Designed for Us.* Prometheus Books, 2011.

Chapter 5: Life Is Life

Bering, Jesse. *The Belief Instinct: The Psychology of Souls, Destiny, and the Meaning of Life.* W. W. Norton, 2011.

Carrier, Richard. *Sense & Goodness Without God: A Defense of Metaphysical Naturalism.* Authorhouse, 2005.

Dawkins, Richard. *Unweaving the Rainbow: Science, Delusion and the Appetite for Wonder.* Mariner Books, 2000.

Dennett, Daniel C., and Linda LaScola. *Caught in The Pulpit: Leaving Belief Behind.* Congruity, 2013.

Johnson, Chris. *A Better Life: 100 Atheists Speak Out on Joy & Meaning in a World Without God.* Cosmic Teapot, 2014.

Lalli, Nica. *Nothing: Something To Believe In.* Prometheus Books, 2007.

Maisel, Eric. *The Atheist's Way: Living Well Without Gods.* New World Library, 2009.

Myers, P. Z. *The Happy Atheist.* Pantheon, 2013.

Zuckerman, Phil. *Society Without God: What the Least Religious Nations Can Tell Us about Contentment.* New York University Press, 2008.

INDEX

ABOUT THE AUTHOR

Dan Barker, a former evangelical minister, is copresident of the Freedom From Religion Foundation (FFRF), cohost of Freethought Radio, and cofounder and board member of The Clergy Project. A widely sought after lecturer, debater, and performer, he regularly discusses atheism and life's meaning and purpose in the national media, with appearances on *The Daily Show*, Oprah Winfrey's *AM Chicago*, *The O'Reilly Factor*, *Good Morning America*, and many others. A professional jazz pianist and songwriter, he has five children and ten grandchildren. He lives in Madison, Wisconsin, with his wife Annie Laurie Gaylor, who is copresident of FFRF.